THE MASTER ARCHITECT SERIES III
MICHAEL GRAVES
Selected and Current Works

THE MASTER ARCHITECT SERIES III
MICHAEL GRAVES
Selected and Current Works

First published in Australia in 1999 by
The Images Publishing Group Pty Ltd
ACN 059 734 431
6 Bastow Place, Mulgrave, Victoria, 3170
Telephone (61 3) 9561 5544 Facsimile (61 3) 9561 4860

National Library of Australia Cataloguing-in-Publication Data

       Michael Graves, 1934–
       Michael Graves: selected and current works.

       Bibliography.
       Includes index.
       ISBN 1 875498 73 7.

       1. Graves, Michael, 1934–Catalogs. 2. Architecture,
       Modern—20th Century—Catalogs. 3. Architects—United
       States—20th Century—Catalogs. I. Title.
       (Series: The master architect series, 1320-7253).

   720.92

Edited by Stephen Dobney
Designed by The Graphic Image Studio Pty Ltd,
Mulgrave, Australia
Film by PageSet Pty. Ltd Australia
Printed in Hong Kong

Contents

Introduction

1

2

3

4

1 The Portland Building
2 The Humana Building
3 Walt Disney World Dolphin Hotel
4 The Team Disney Building

Introduction

Michael Graves, the Media, and the Making of Metonymic Architecture
By Christian Zapatka

A recent television news clip described a potential takeover of Humana, Inc., headquartered in Louisville, Kentucky, by another even larger corporation. Curiously, the clip showed no people, no charts, no frantic transactions; instead, it focused on the building that the company had built for itself in 1985. The camera lingered on the company's name etched into the green marble above the front door and then featured various views of the building from the street and from the skyline. The views showed the seven-story porch-like base of the building in alignment with its neighboring smaller-scale buildings; its slab-shaped shaft, clad in pink granite, stepped back, rising above that level in a separate gesture; and its top, marked by a swelling band of stone under which a bracket of intricately articulated structural bracing holds a sky porch offering views of the Ohio River.

The metonymy (the use of the name of one thing for that of another suggested by or associated with it) is striking here. The Humana Building itself stands for the company, and, to a certain extent, for the city as well, since the image of the building has given the skyline of Louisville an unmistakable identity. This news clip illustrated how a building, commissioned as a company headquarters, can assume more than the purely functional role of a typical office building. The building is now emblematic of the company and a dominating mark on the Louisville skyline. The corporation housed in the building is perceptible to the public more because of the building it occupies than because of an understanding of the business of the company.

The Humana Building, designed by Michael Graves for an international competition in 1982, followed quickly on the heels of another competition he had won in 1980. This earlier commission resulted in the highly controversial Portland Building, which is now universally recognized as an icon of Postmodernism and which turned a Princeton University professor into an overnight sensation. This civic building, a simple box transformed by a giant-scale cloak of color and pattern based on historical architectural elements, gave to the city of Portland, Oregon, a striking architectural identity, which now shows up on T-shirts advertising the city—another case of metonymic architecture.

Following Portland and Humana came the equally iconic Walt Disney World hotels (1987) in Orlando, Florida, and the Disney Corporate Headquarters (1986) in Burbank, California, along with a host of other corporate and institutional structures which have subsequently resulted in commissions for dozens of buildings of all sizes around the globe, too numerous to list here.

The Dolphin and Swan hotels near Walt Disney World are, of course, classically metonymic, with their respectively 60- and 46-foot-high figural representations marking the presence of the hotels—and thus Walt Disney World itself—from a great distance. Intentionally designed to appeal to the masses of people—adults as well as children—who make Walt Disney World a mecca, these monumentally scaled figures can also be understood within a historical context of oversized figures signifying place: the sphinxes in Egypt, the Colossus at Rhodes, the fictional Trojan Horse, the Elephant of 19th century Paris.

The Humana Building

Design/Completion 1982/1985
Louisville, Kentucky
Humana, Inc.
525,000 square feet
Steel frame
Granite

The Humana Building, a 26-story office tower in downtown Louisville, Kentucky, is the headquarters for a well-known American company specializing in health care. The modern buildings surrounding the site are set back from the street on plazas, eroding the historical urban street wall pattern. In contrast, the Humana Building occupies its entire site and re-establishes the street edge as an essential urban form. The building's contextual relationship with this particular city and site is reinforced by its orientation toward the Ohio River and its mediation of the scale difference between the small townhouses on one side and the office tower on the other.

The 525,000-square-foot building includes two parking levels below grade, retail shops on the first floor, and offices and a conference center above. The building's formal organization reflects its division into these significant parts. The lower portion, six stories high, is devoted to public space and to Humana's executive offices. General offices are located in the body of the building. The conference center occupies the 25th floor, with access to a large outdoor porch overlooking the city and the river beyond.

1

2

1   View from the Ohio River
2   View from Main Street
3   Twenty-fifth floor balcony
4   View from the southeast

3

4

5

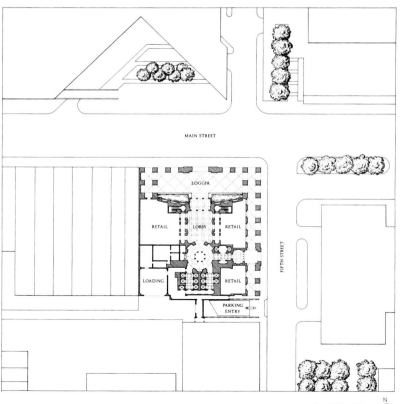

5   Twenty-fifth floor terrace
6   Site plan
Opposite:
   View from Main Street

6

9

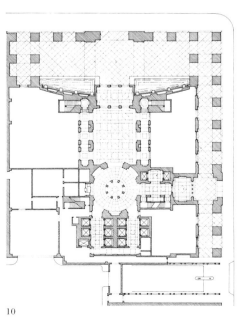

10

11

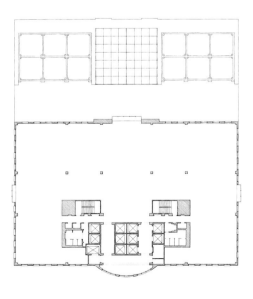

12

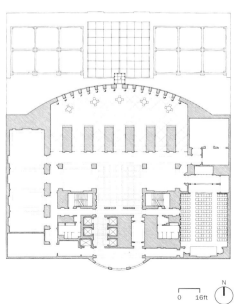

13

Far left:
    Fifth Street loggia
9   Elevator lobby
10 First floor plan
11 Public loggia
12 Typical office floor plan
13 Conference center plan

0 16ft   N

15

16

14   Sixth floor reception
15   Entrance lobby
16   First floor rotunda

The Crown American Building

Design/Completion 1986/1989
Johnstown, Pennsylvania
Crown American Corporation
130,000 square feet
Steel frame
Kasota stone, bluestone

The corporate headquarters for Crown American Corporation is a four-story, 130,000-square-foot building organized around a central atrium. The building's exterior character responds to the diverse institutional context of the immediate surroundings. The design vocabulary is reflected in the polychromatic values of the stone facades, in the roof forms, and in the two entrance pavilions developed to accommodate the irregular corner site. One is a rotunda of columns that serves as a porch for community events; the other is a truncated pyramid that serves as a porte-cochere for vehicular drop-off.

The skylit upper levels of the pyramidal structure contain Crown American's executive offices and library. The interiors incorporate many custom-designed furnishings. For the dining room, Graves composed the "Archaic Landscape" mural and designed the furniture, light fixtures, carpet, and corporate china.

1

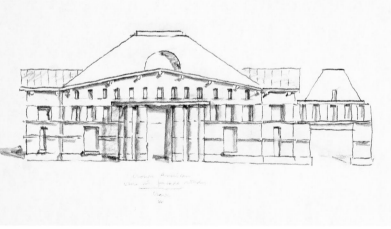

2

3

24

1   View from the southeast
2   Vine Street elevation study
3   View from the southeast
4   View from the northeast

4

The Crown American Building   25

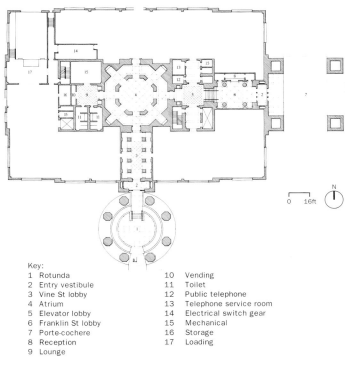

Key:
1	Rotunda	10	Vending
2	Entry vestibule	11	Toilet
3	Vine St lobby	12	Public telephone
4	Atrium	13	Telephone service room
5	Elevator lobby	14	Electrical switch gear
6	Franklin St lobby	15	Mechanical
7	Porte-cochere	16	Storage
8	Reception	17	Loading
9	Lounge		

6

7

5 Franklin Street entrance lobby
6 Ground floor plan
7 Atrium

8

9

11

12

8   Executive suite passage
9   Executive suite rotunda
Middle:
      Upper level of library in executive suite rotunda
11 Corporate boardroom
12 Executive office
Following pages:
      Executive dining room

10 Peachtree Place

Design/Completion 1987/1991
Atlanta, Georgia
L.J. Hooker (developer), Coca-Cola
Corporation (owner)
300,000 square feet (total floor area)
Reinforced concrete
Red granite

This 20-story, 300,000-square-foot office building, now a computer center for the Coca Cola Corporation, is adjacent to a nine-story hotel and a rapid transit station connecting midtown Atlanta to the city's larger metropolitan region. The main facade of the building faces south, centered on West Peachtree Street, a major axis through downtown Atlanta. The building is entered through an open, three-story arcade on this facade. Clad in three varieties of Cippolino marble, the main public lobbies connect retail and commercial space on the first two floors. A loggia surrounds the top floor adjacent to common conference facilities.

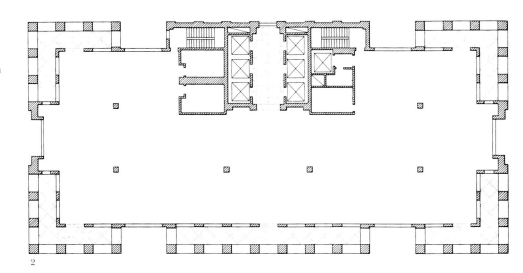

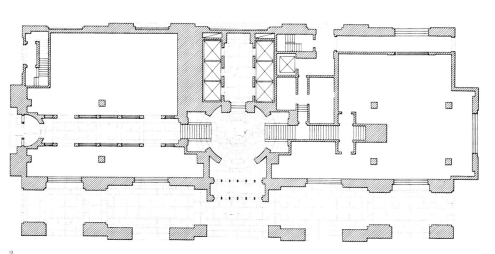

1 Second floor rotunda lobby
2 Thirteenth to sixteenth floor plan
3 Second floor plan
4 View from the south

4

Tajima Office Building

Design/Completion 1988/1993
Tokyo, Japan
Tajima Corporation Ltd.
50,000 square feet
Steel, reinforced concrete
Glazed tile

This nine-story urban infill office building is located in Tokyo on the banks of the Kanda River. In addition to Tajima's corporate offices, the building contains a showroom for the company's tile product line. The building has its own identity, yet its design respects the street wall created by surrounding buildings. The upper portion of the building is composed of a stacked colonnade that utilizes a pattern of blue and white tiles in response to the building's waterfront location. Large windows on the higher levels provide views of Tokyo.

1   Terrace detail
2   Entrance facade study
3   Entrance facade detail
4   View from the Kanda River
5   Entrance facade

1

2

3

4

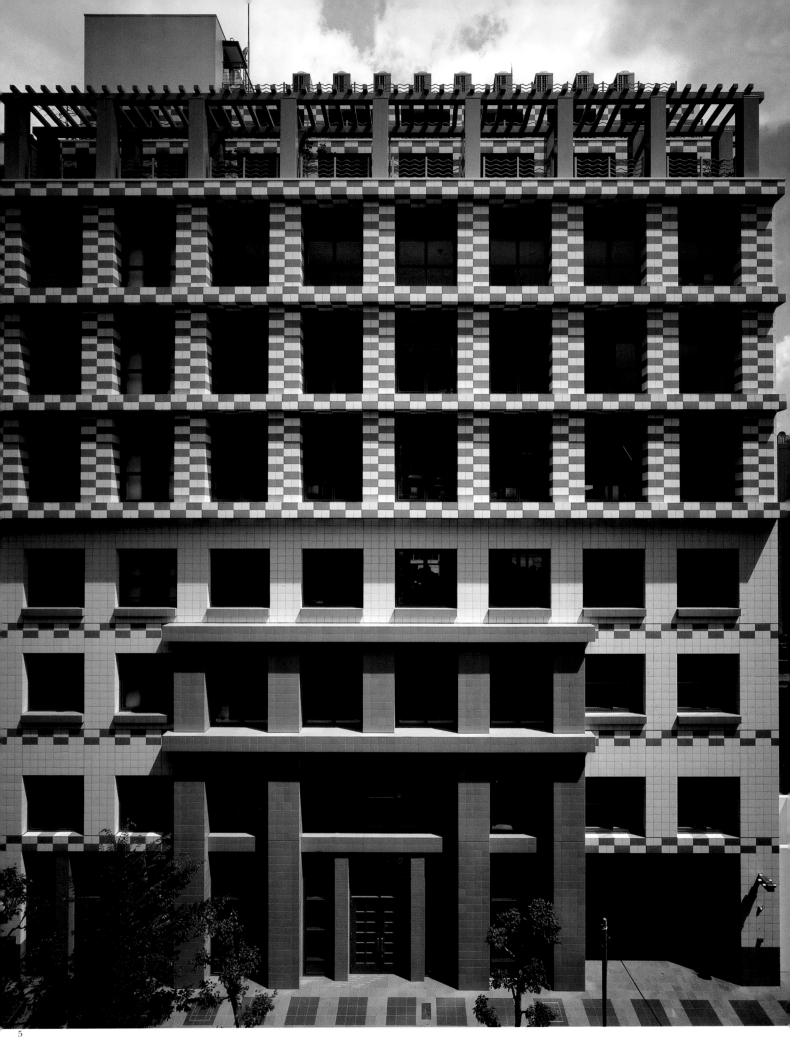

5

7

Opposite:
Ground floor reception
7 Public stair

Kasumi Research and Training Center

Design/Completion 1990/1994
Tsukuba City, Japan
Kasumi Co., Ltd.
113,000 square feet
Steel, reinforced concrete
Glazed tile

1

The program for Kasumi's Research and Training Center includes offices, meeting and training rooms, research facilities, an employee dining room, a tea room, and a gallery. Zoning guidelines dictated the footprint and general massing of the building. To offset the constraints of the zoning envelope, Graves created a fresh architectural character by varying the roof forms and the articulation and coloration of the ceramic tile walls.

Organized in four parts, the building is entered through a cylindrical porte-cochere with a gallery at its upper level. The six-story office building at the center of the composition contains employee research and training functions. Executive offices are located on the top floor to take advantage of views to the surrounding landscape. The smaller volumes to either side of the central block balance the composition. The two-story barrel-vaulted structure to the west contains flexible meeting rooms of different sizes. The two-story truncated structure on the east contains study rooms and a tea room.

1 Detail of meeting room pavilion
   and porte-cochere
2 View from the southwest
Following pages:
   East facade

2

38

4

5

6

4 West facade
5&6 Entrance facade detail
7 Reception lobby

7

Thomson Consumer Electronics Americas Headquarters

Design/Completion 1992/1994
Indianapolis, Indiana
Thomson Consumer Electronics
210,000 square feet (total area)
Steel frame
Colored precast concrete

1

The Americas Headquarters of the international corporation Thomson Consumer Electronics consists of two buildings: an administration building and a technical research and development building sited nearby. Graves joined another architectural firm after the building was under construction to design the cubic central pavilion and atrium of the administration building, to establish the color and pattern of the facades, and to provide interior design services.

Within the central pavilion, a skylit cylindrical atrium and grand stair articulate a "building within a building" that rises through all four stories, creating a dramatic entry sequence and a common forum for the building's occupants. From the grand atrium, visitors may go to the fourth floor exhibition galleries where Thomson's product lines and their historical collection of early model televisions and radios are displayed.

1   Rear facade detail
2   Entrance facade detail
3   Entrance facade
4   Rear facade: approach from parking

2

3

4

Thomson Consumer Electronics Americas Headquarters 45

5

6

8

7

9

5   Facade detail
6&7 Atrium
8   Facade detail
9   Fourth floor gallery
10 Atrium stair

International Finance Corporation Headquarters

Design/Completion 1993/1997
Washington, D.C.
International Finance Corporation of the World Bank Group
1,000,000 square feet
Reinforced concrete

The headquarters of the World Bank Group's International Finance Corporation is located on a triangular site on Pennsylvania Avenue at Washington Circle in Washington, D.C. The program for the 1,000,000-square-foot building includes offices, a training and conference center, a multi-purpose auditorium, a library, and a cafeteria.

The 12-story building reflects the traditional architecture of historic Washington, and yet provides a fresh approach to classical organization. Following the cornice height typical of surrounding blocks, the major facades are subdivided and articulated with a variety of window types to offer relief along their 600-foot length. A series of pavilions pulled forward from the body of the building help break down the scale of the long facades on Pennsylvania Avenue and K Street, and provide opportunities to plan many corner offices. A cylindrical belvedere turns the corner at Washington Circle, affording views in all directions.

1

1 View from Pennsylvania Avenue
  and 21st Street
2 View from Washington Circle along
  Pennsylvania Avenue

2

Opposite:
Atrium
4 Entrance lobby
5 Entrance lobby reception

4

RECEPTION

5

6　Typical floor plan
7　North lobby leading to auditorium
8　North–south section
9　Auditorium

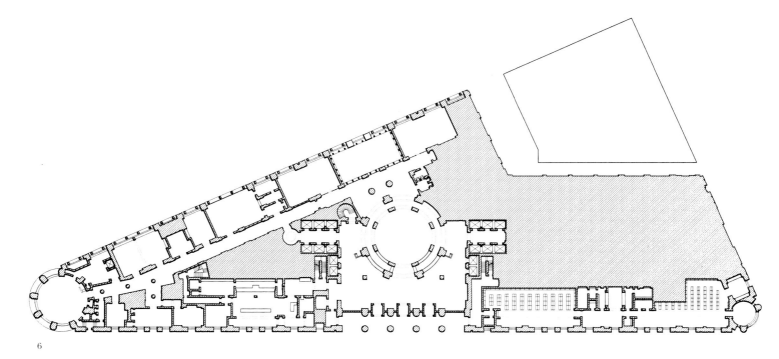

6

7

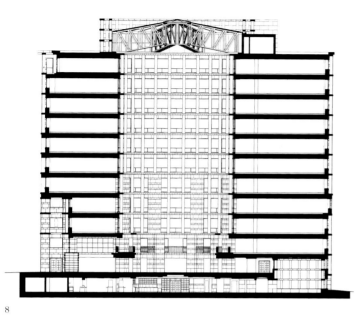

8

9

10 Private dining room
11 Credit union
12 Cafeteria

10

11

12

Castalia

Design/Completion 1993/1998
The Hague, Holland
MAB bv
29,215 square meters
Existing jack-slab construction
Sandstone, cast stone with glazed brick bay windows, copper roof,
brick annexes

Castalia is one part of a redevelopment master plan for de Resident, a mixed-use section of The Hague that includes office buildings and housing. This project involves recladding an existing jack-slab building from the 1950s and developing two annexes along Zwarteweg: one forming a gate to a new courtyard, and the other completing the street facade between the Transitorium and Zurich Tower, an adjacent new office building. The Transitorium will house offices for the Ministry of Health, Welfare and Sport.

The design strategy for Castalia reconciles the small scale of low-rise housing with the larger scale of surrounding high-rise office buildings, partly by referring to traditional Dutch architectural elements. The articulation of the building as twin "towers" separated by protruding glazed brick bay windows reinforces a new vertical reading of the building and recalls Dutch roof forms. The new building facades accommodate the structural constraints of the existing building and reflect the typical articulation of Dutch windows, which is evident in several nearby examples.

2

3

1

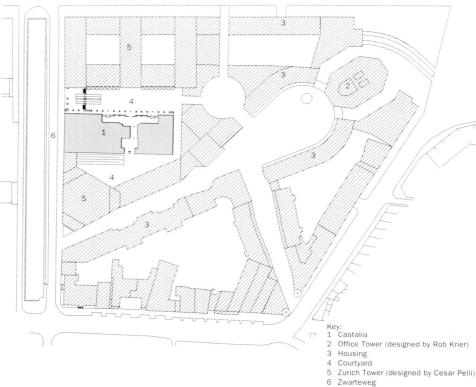

4

Key:
1 Castalia
2 Office Tower (designed by Rob Krier)
3 Housing
4 Courtyard
5 Zurich Tower (designed by Cesar Pelli)
6 Zwarteweg

0   5   10m

N

1 View of de Resident development with existing
   Transitorium building to right of center
2 Courtyard facade
3 Zwarteweg facade
4 Site plan
5 Preliminary model: view from Zwarteweg

5

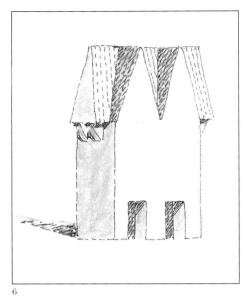

6

7

8

9

10

11

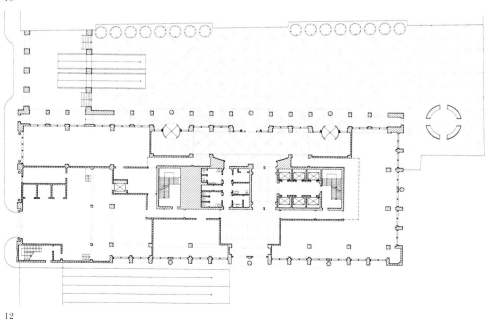

12

13

14

15

16

6–8　Character studies
9　Construction photograph
10　Ground floor plan
11　Typical floor plan
12　Construction view
13–15　View from canal
16　Lobby

Castalia　59

Delaware River Port Authority

Design/Completion 1994/1996
Camden, New Jersey
Delaware River Port Authority
176,000 square feet
Steel frame
Colored precast concrete, glazed brick

1

2

The headquarters of the Delaware River Port Authority of New Jersey and Pennsylvania (DRPA) is one of the cornerstones of the Camden waterfront redevelopment. The L-shaped site overlooks the Delaware River and offers spectacular views toward Philadelphia. The site also flanks an existing parking garage at the center of the block; a future companion building will be developed on the opposite side of the garage.

The 176,000-square-foot, 11-story building includes retail shops and a restaurant at the base, four floors of leased office space, and six floors of headquarters offices for the DRPA. The executive offices and boardroom are located on the top floor of the building behind yellow, three-story aluminum columns.

A two-story loggia across the base extends in front of the existing garage. A proposed colonnade centered on the garage reinstalls two large, winged victory sculptures designed by the Philadelphia architect Paul Cret for the approaches to the Ben Franklin Bridge, thereby linking the new headquarters building to the past achievements of the Authority.

3

1 Entrance elevation: DRPA headquarters and future building
2 Main entrance, Riverside Drive facade
3 Federal Street facade
4 Riverside Drive facade

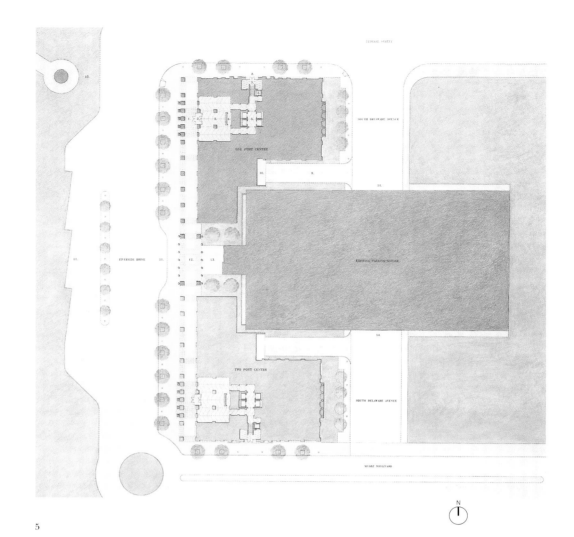

5

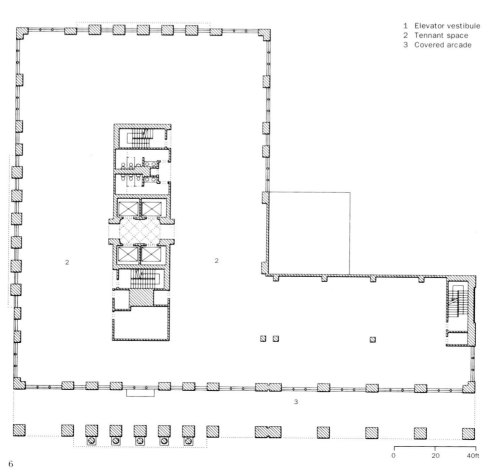

1 Elevator vestibule
2 Tennant space
3 Covered arcade

6

0   20   40ft

7

5   Site plan: DRPA to the south of parking garage
    and future building to the north
6   Second floor plan
7   Boardroom

World Trade Exchange Center

Design 1996
Manila, Philippines
Empire State Land, Inc.
45,000 square meters
Poured-in-place concrete
Stone, stucco, metal louvers

The World Trade Exchange Center is a
mixed-use building 35 stories high, located
in Metro Manila's historic district near
Manila Bay and the Pasig River. The
massing, fenestration patterns, and
coloration articulate the various uses of
the building. The base contains two floors
of retail space above which are six floors
of parking with openings shielded by
awning-like metal louvers. The upper
portion of the building, used principally
for offices, is divided into two sections to
help diminish the scale of the building in
deference to its mid-rise neighbors. The
cylindrical corner tower with its large
expanse of windows faces Manila Bay.

1

2

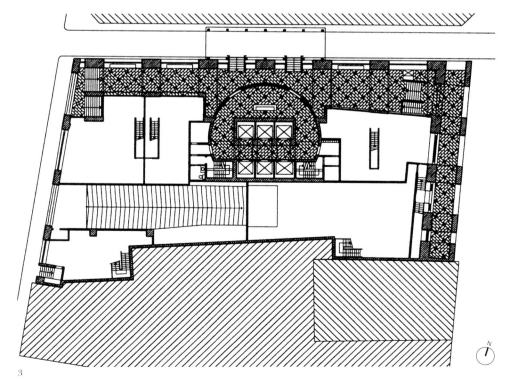

3

1   Site plan
2   Elevation study
3   Ground floor plan
4   Model: view from Calle Muelle de Binondo
5   Function room
6   Calle Muelle de Binondo elevation
7   Calle Ninfa elevation
8   Promenade

4

5

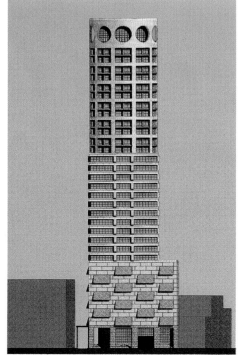

6

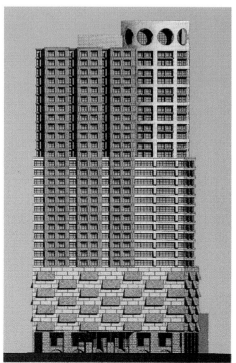

7

8

Fujian Xingye Banking Tower

Design 1996
Shanghai, China
Fujian Xingye Bank
55,000 square meters
Reinforced concrete
Stone

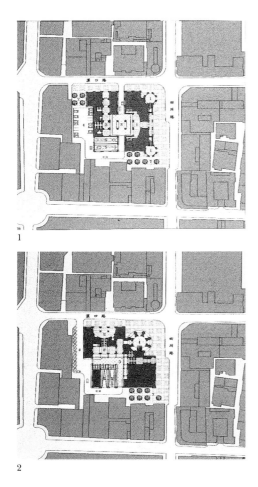

1

2

The Fujian Xingye tower is a 26-story mixed-use building located in the historic district of Shanghai near the Courthouse and Customs Building and facing the Bund. The lower 10 floors contain banking facilities as well as retail and office space, while the tower contains tenant office space. These different functions are expressed through massing, architectural design, materials and colors.

1 Site plan, scheme 1
2 Site plan, scheme 2
3 Front elevation, scheme 1
4 Front elevation, scheme 2
5 Side elevation, scheme 1
6 Side elevation, scheme 2

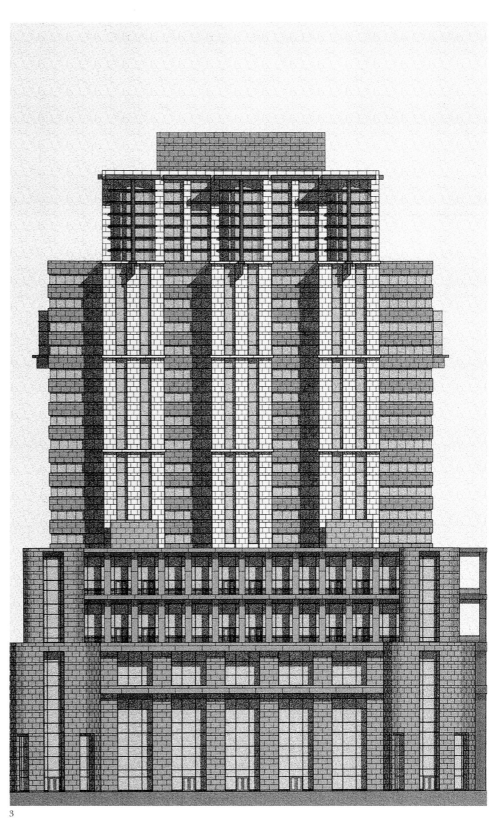

3

4

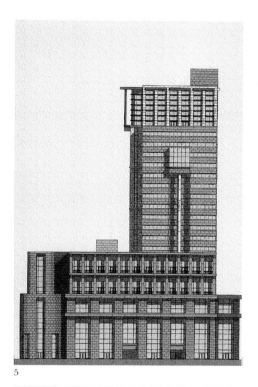

5

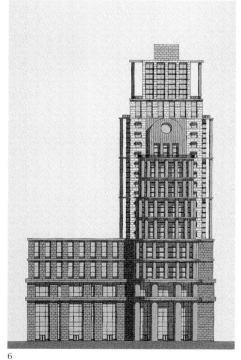

6

Miele Americas Headquarters

Design 1996
Princeton, New Jersey
Miele Appliances, Inc.
31,400 square feet
Steel frame
Brick, glazed block, aluminum panels

1

The Americas headquarters of this international company specializing in high-quality household appliances is located on the Route One highway, so it was essential that the building design address the passing high-speed traffic. The first floor accommodates a large showroom to welcome visitors and provide display areas for various Miele products. A double-height portion of the showroom is enclosed in glass, allowing the space to be flooded with natural light during the day and becoming a glowing landmark at night. Surrounding the showroom are various spaces associated with the presentation of Miele products, including a reception area, a training room, demonstration stations, and meeting rooms. The second floor is used for Miele's offices.

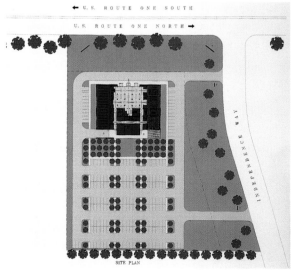

2

3

1 Route One elevation
2 Site plan
3 Construction view

NCAA 2000 Headquarters and Hall of Champions

Design 1997
Indianapolis, Indiana
White River State Park Development
Commission
180,000 square feet
Steel frame
Brick, copper

The headquarters office building, conference center, and Hall of Champions for the National Collegiate Athletic Association (NCAA) occupies a prominent site on the Central Canal in White River State Park in Indianapolis. The composition of the complex as a series of interconnected structures creates a campus-like setting which both reflects the character of the park and makes reference to the collegiate atmosphere of the NCAA's member institutions.

The 140,000-square-foot program for the offices and conference center is accommodated in a four-story barrel-vaulted block on the northern part of the site. The conference center is located on the ground floor contiguous to the main entrance and the 40,000-square-foot Hall of Champions. Offices are located primarily on the upper floors around a full-height atrium overlooking the entrance plaza and the park.

The simplicity of the office building's mass and articulation allows it to serve as a backdrop to the more specialized features of the project: the semi-circular plan of the Hall of Champions exhibit center to the west and the Acme Evans Superintendent's Building to the east, which is a historic building on the site to be renovated for the NCAA library and visitor services. The building complex thus locates the two emphases of the NCAA—athletic achievement and academic pursuit—to either side of the central outdoor courtyard. The courtyard provides a common open space that extends the main greensward of the park and links the new complex to its surroundings.

1

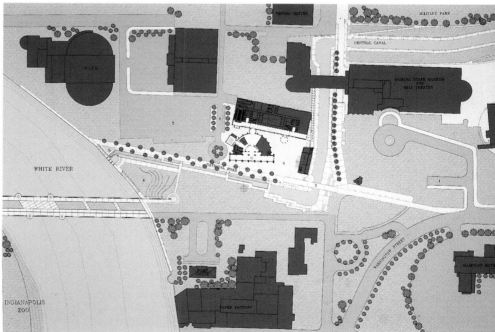
2

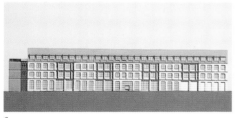

3

4

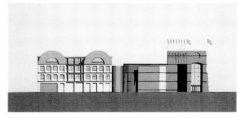

5

1   View of Hall of Champions and entrance
2   Site plan
3   Rear elevation
4   Central Canal elevation
5   White River elevation

6

7

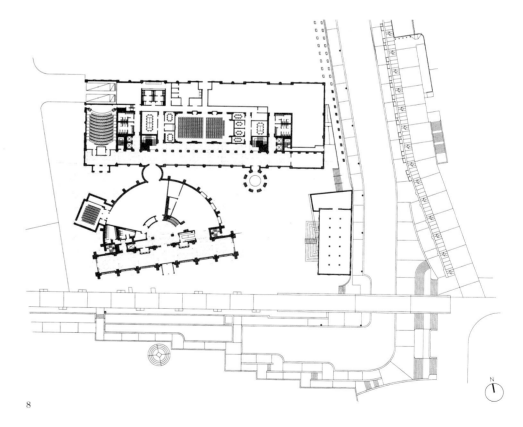

8

6   White River facade
7   Entrance elevation
8   Ground floor plan
9   Atrium

9

Fortis/AG Headquarters

Design 1997
Brussels, Belgium
Fortis/AG
36,700 square meters in two buildings
Concrete
Stone, copper roof

1

2

The headquarters office building for the Belgian insurance company Fortis/AG is located at 53 Boulevard Emile Jacqmain in the heart of the historic old pentagon of Brussels. In response to the traditional nature of the context, the design is reminiscent of characteristically Belgian facade rhythms, materials, and detailing, but at the same time presents a fresh and contemporary public image for the company.

The 112-meter-long facade along Boulevard Emile Jacqmain is articulated as a series of vertical elements or pavilions which offset the large size of the building and help it relate to the human scale of the city. Entryways to the building and expansive windows are provided between the pavilions through more delicate architectural frames.

The base, body, and upper stories of the building, and the reclad building at number 83 which will house its future expansion, recall the traditional three-part composition of the prevalent local architecture. The window detailing and the materials—bluestone base, intermediate stone coursing, and cream-colored limestone facades—are also similar to local examples. Terracing back from the streetwall, the upper floors of number 53 recall the dormered roofs of neighboring buildings. A cylindrical tower at the corner of Rue St. Michel, similar to that of the adjacent building, will feature Fortis's logotype.

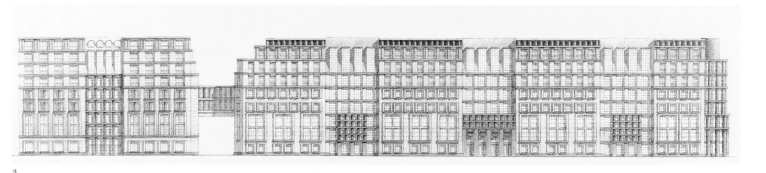

3

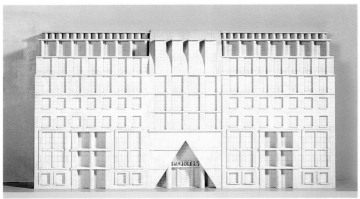

1   View from Boulevard Emile Jacqmain
2   Perspective view from Boulevard Emile Jacqmain
3   Boulevard Emile Jacqmain elevation
4   Competition phase partial facade model

4

Hotels, Recreation and Commercial

The Aventine

Design/Completion 1985/1990
La Jolla, California
The Naiman Company
1.2 million square feet
Steel frame
Red Barouli sandstone base, cream-colored stucco top

1

2

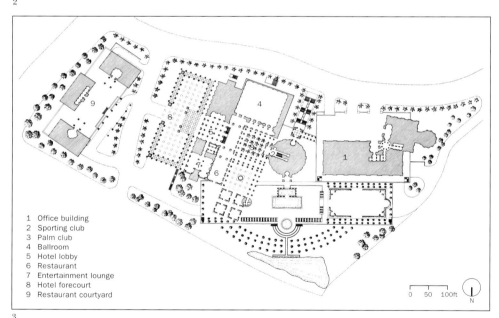

1 Office building
2 Sporting club
3 Palm club
4 Ballroom
5 Hotel lobby
6 Restaurant
7 Entertainment lounge
8 Hotel forecourt
9 Restaurant courtyard

0   50   100ft

N

3

4

The Aventine is a mixed-use development located on a 12-acre site in University Center, La Jolla, California. The program included a 400-room Hyatt Regency hotel, a 225,000-square-foot office building, a health club with outdoor swimming pool, a compound of five restaurants, and extensive underground parking. The buildings are sited to take advantage of the southern view and to allow sunlight to penetrate to the center of the site where outdoor recreational activities are located.

Although the buildings have their own identities, the commonality of their architectural language, coloration, and materials allows The Aventine to be recognized as a unified ensemble. The hotel's interiors were all designed by Graves and include numerous custom-designed furnishings.

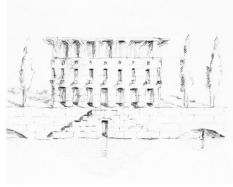

5

6

7

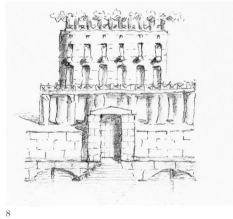

8

1   Hotel facade detail
2   View from the north
3   Site plan
4   Hyatt Regency entrance
5–8 Health club rotunda study

9–11 Hotel details
12 Restaurant pavilion and courtyard

9

10

11

12

14

15

16

8

9

10

Opposite:
    Working court
8   Courtyard facade
9   Winery view from entry portico
10 View of fermentation shed from entry portico

Opposite:
Fermentation shed, interior view

Clos Pegase Winery 89

Walt Disney World® Resort Dolphin Hotel
Walt Disney World® Resort Swan Hotel

Design/Completion 1987/1990
Walt Disney World Resort, Florida
The Walt Disney Company, Tishman Realty
& Construction Company
2 million square feet
Reinforced concrete and steel superstructure
Exterior insulation and finish system with
painted murals

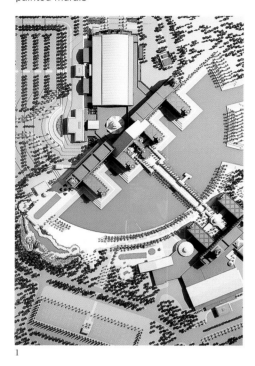

1

The 1,500-room Walt Disney World Resort Dolphin Hotel faces its companion project, the 758-room Walt Disney World Resort Swan Hotel, across a large crescent-shaped artificial lake. Both hotels contain extensive convention facilities, restaurants, and retail shops.

The colors and decorations of the two hotels suggest the character of Florida resorts and provide a thematic context consistent with Disney's program for "entertainment architecture." Gigantic statues of dolphins and swans mark the ends of the hotel roofs, making the hotels visible and recognizable from a great distance. Within both hotels, the lobbies, ballrooms, guestroom corridors, restaurants, and other areas experienced by hotel visitors are embellished by a wide variety of patterned materials and custom-designed light fixtures and furniture, delighting the visitor with the unexpected.

1   Site model
2   Dolphin Hotel from Crescent Lake

2

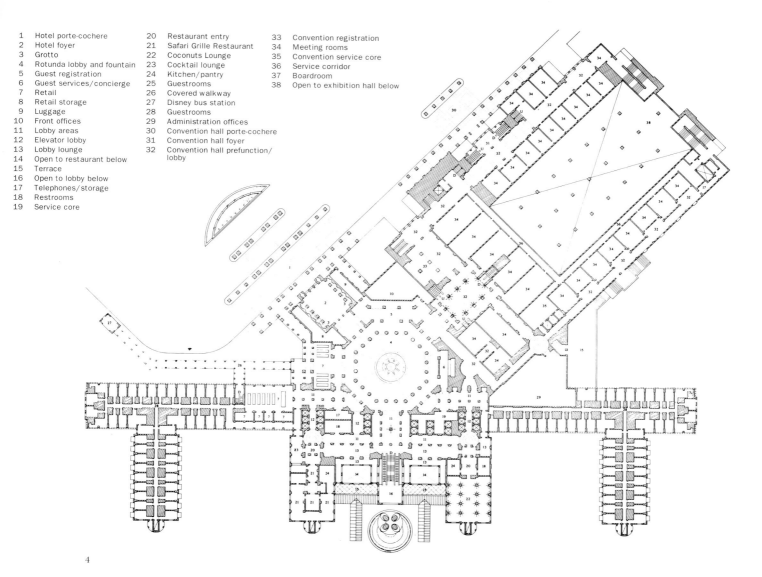

1   Hotel porte-cochere
2   Hotel foyer
3   Grotto
4   Rotunda lobby and fountain
5   Guest registration
6   Guest services/concierge
7   Retail
8   Retail storage
9   Luggage
10 Front offices
11 Lobby areas
12 Elevator lobby
13 Lobby lounge
14 Open to restaurant below
15 Terrace
16 Open to lobby below
17 Telephones/storage
18 Restrooms
19 Service core
20 Restaurant entry
21 Safari Grille Restaurant
22 Coconuts Lounge
23 Cocktail lounge
24 Kitchen/pantry
25 Guestrooms
26 Covered walkway
27 Disney bus station
28 Guestrooms
29 Administration offices
30 Convention hall porte-cochere
31 Convention hall foyer
32 Convention hall prefunction/lobby
33 Convention registration
34 Meeting rooms
35 Convention service core
36 Service corridor
37 Boardroom
38 Open to exhibition hall below

4

5

6

Opposite:
   Dolphin Hotel facade
4 Dolphin Hotel third floor plan
5 Dolphin Hotel guestroom corridor
6 Dolphin Hotel typical guestroom

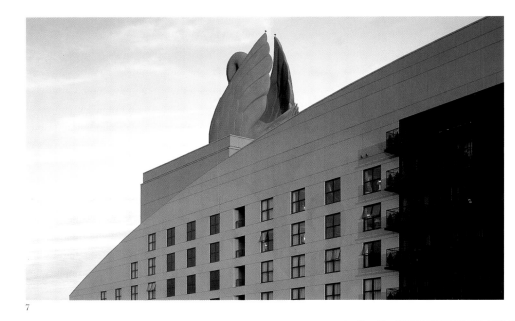

7

Opposite:
  Pyramidal skylight above hotel lobby
6   Hotel rotunda lobby with pyramidal skylight
Following pages:
  Hotel lobby lounge

6

8

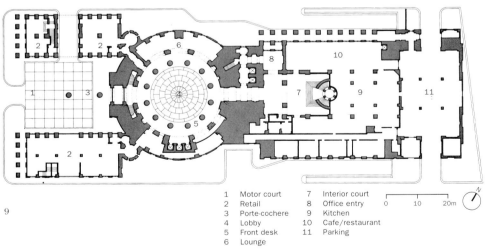

1	Motor court	7	Interior court
2	Retail	8	Office entry
3	Porte-cochere	9	Kitchen
4	Lobby	10	Cafe/restaurant
5	Front desk	11	Parking
6	Lounge		

0   10   20m

9

8   Typical hotel guestroom
9   Ground floor plan
10   Second floor hotel rotunda
11   Gold-leafed stair from hotel to office building
     atrium

10

4

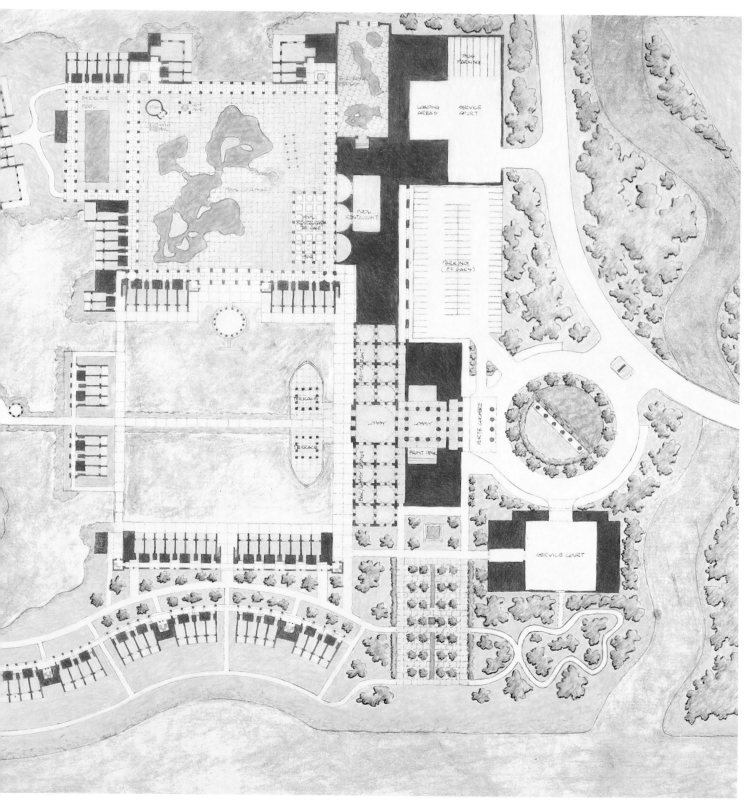

5

6

7

5   Character study
6   Entrance facade, main hotel
7   Red Sea facade, main hotel

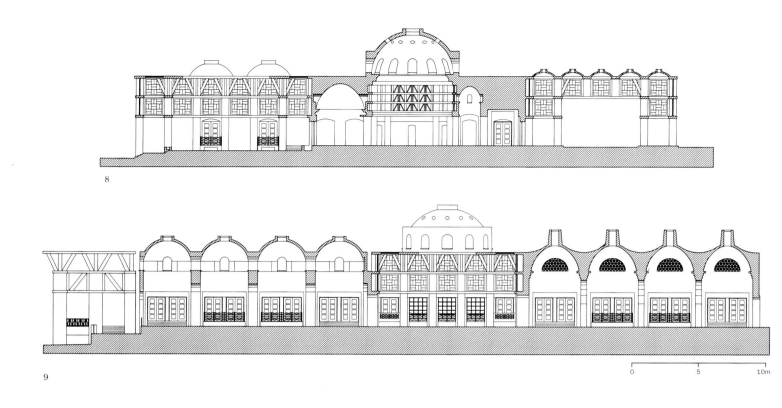

8

9

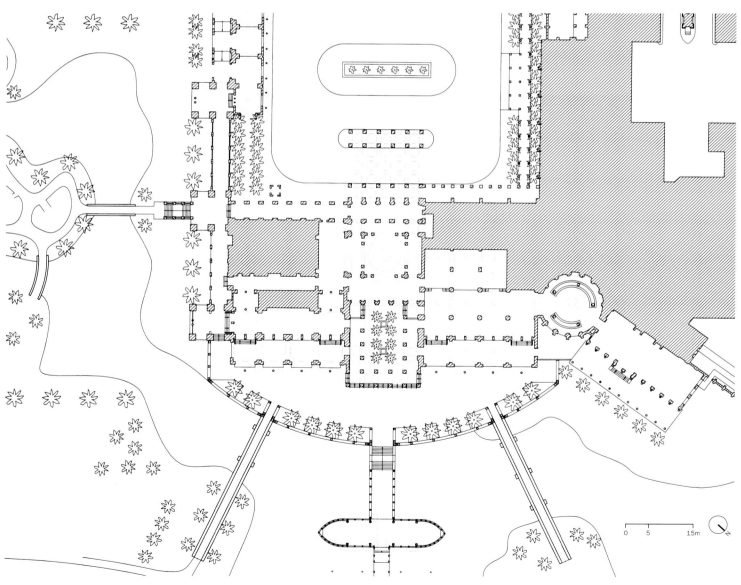

10

11

12

8   Main hotel section through lobby
9   Main hotel section through restaurant and
     Palm Court
10   Main hotel plan
11   Restaurant
12   Hotel lobby
13   Hotel passage
14   Hotel bar
15   Shaded walkway to hotel

13

14

15

16

17

18

19

20

21

22

23

24

25

26

27

28

29

4

6

7

8

Opposite:
  Grand stair
6 Reception hall
7 Mezzanine gallery surrounding reception hall
8 Reception hall

Ortigas Tycoon Twin Towers

Design 1996
Ortigas, Philippines
Amberland Corporation
1.2 million square feet
Poured-in-place concrete
Stone, curtain wall

The Ortigas Tycoon Twin Towers is a mixed-use development consisting of two 38-story towers, one of which contains office space and the other a condominium hotel. The towers are situated above a common six-story podium containing retail, recreational, and parking facilities. Several alternative schemes were studied to provide a variety of fenestration options.

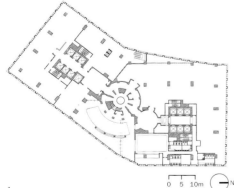

0 5 10m

1

ORTIGAS TYCOON CENTRE

2

3

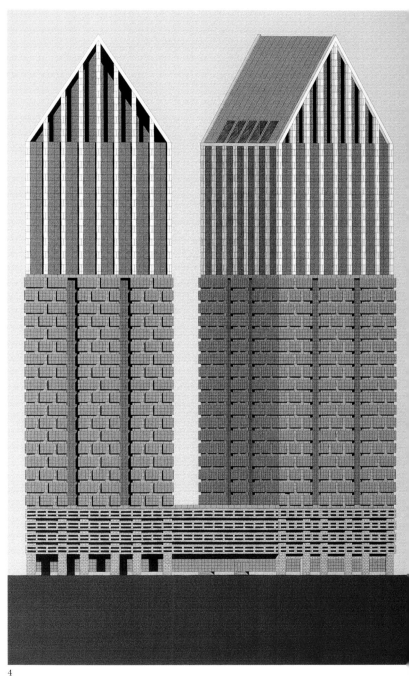

4

1   Plan
2   Pearl Street elevation, scheme 1
3   Pearl Street elevation, scheme 2
4   Pearl Street elevation, scheme 3

Cotton Bay Resort Hotel

Competition 1998
Eleuthera, Bahamas
Cotton Bay Holdings Ltd.
304,000 square feet (total area)
Reinforced concrete, masonry bearing wall
Stone, stucco, wood

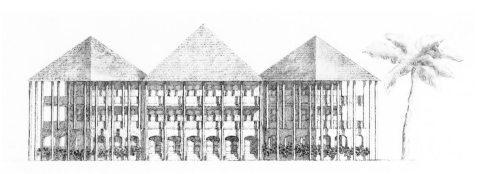

1

The design of the Cotton Bay Resort Hotel emphasizes the relationship between buildings and the natural landscape, including the bay and the adjacent golf course. The western portion of the site would be developed in an initial phase and the eastern portion at a later time. The hotel is developed as a series of individual buildings oriented toward the bay and landscape features such as pools and gardens.

The U-shaped 64-room main hotel building is organized around a formal landscaped courtyard onto which face various public facilities such as the bar, restaurants, and banquet hall. Above the public rooms rise seven stories of guest rooms in a single-loaded corridor configuration that affords views of the bay from every room. The remaining guest rooms are organized in two arc-shaped buildings centered on a landscaped swimming pool and the beach. This organizational strategy provides a sense of community at a domestic scale while preserving the privacy of individual quarters.

Throughout the resort, the buildings have been given a quiet elegance through their traditional architectural character with vernacular associations. Exterior materials are whitewashed rough stone with wood treillage, shutters, and louvers. To complement the calm and quiet nature of the buildings, the landscaping would create an informal, natural tropical environment of indigenous vegetation such as palm trees, climbing vines, and flowers.

2

3

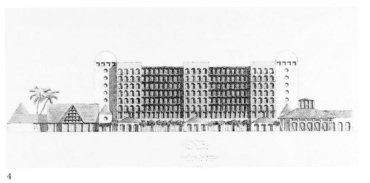

4

1 Guestroom group H, typical elevation
2 Specialty restaurant 2, beachfront elevation
3 Site plan
4 Main hotel building, beachfront elevation
5 Specialty restaurant 1, beachfront elevation

5

Peek & Cloppenburg Department Store

Design 1998
Dusseldorf, Germany
Peek und Cloppenburg AG
100,000 square feet
Reinforced concrete
Cast stone, limestone, curtain wall

Graves' competition entry for a department store for one of Germany's largest clothing companies reflects its dynamic urban surroundings and makes the internal retail displays visible to the passerby. The site, located on Schadowstrasse, the city's most prominent shopping street, is greatly influenced by an adjacent elevated highway, the landmark Berliner Allee. Two glass pylons, one developed at the most prominent corner of the building and the other located directly across the street, form a prominent gateway in the city and provide a well-lit showcase for general merchandise and special promotions.

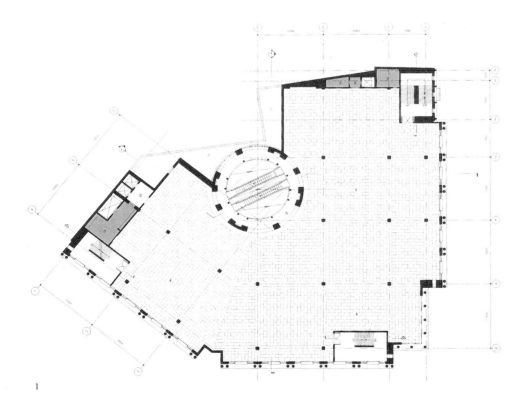

1

1   Schematic design: third and fourth floor plans
2   Schematic design drawing: night view from Schadowstrasse
3   Preliminary elevation

2

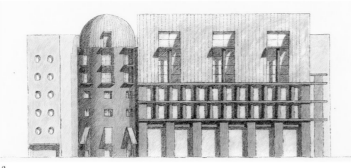

3

4

5

4 Schematic design model
5 Schematic design model: view from Berliner Allee

Cultural and Civic

The Newark Museum

Design/Completion 1982/1989
Newark, New Jersey
The Newark Museum
175,000 square feet (renovation area)
Steel frame
Stucco on new facades

1

The Newark Museum represents the fields of art, science, and industry and offers extensive education programs and services to the community. Michael Graves has been the architect for the museum since 1967, when he prepared the first of three master plans for its renovation and expansion. Located on Washington Park in downtown Newark, the museum comprises several interconnected buildings designed at different times for different purposes: the Main Building, designed specifically for the museum in the 1920s by Jarvis Hunt; the South Wing, a former YWCA premises; the Ballantine House, a Victorian mansion; and the North Wing, a former office building and warehouse built in two phases in the 1940s.

The project illustrated here is a renovation of the Main Building, South Wing and North Wing to accommodate galleries for the permanent collections of art, an auditorium, educational facilities, a mini-zoo, a planetarium, collection storage, and administrative offices. Fundamental to the plan are three skylit courts linked by gallery passages. The original museum court remains at the center of the composition, while a new, three-story skylit sculpture court connects the Main Building, the North Wing, and Ballantine House. The third skylit space, the entrance lobby to the South Wing, leads visitors to the auditorium on the lower level or to galleries and Education Department facilities on upper levels.

2

1 View from Washington Street
2 South Wing entrance
3 American Sculpture Gallery

3

4

5

6

7

4 Auditorium
5 American Art Gallery
6 Asian Art Gallery
7 Decorative Arts Pavilion

Michael C. Carlos Museum

Design/Completion 1990/1993
Atlanta, Georgia
Emory University
35,000 square feet (total floor area)
Steel frame
Georgia marble, clay tile roof

The Michael C. Carlos Museum is connected to a historic building on Emory University's original quadrangle that was designed by Pittsburgh architect Henry Hornbostel as a law school and was subsequently renovated by Graves for the museum and two academic departments. The site marks the cross-axis of the quadrangle, so the central entrance pavilion serves as a backdrop to university-wide gatherings held in this grand outdoor space. The architectural character of the new building is sympathetic to its context in massing, scale, and materials.

First floor galleries for the permanent collection of ancient art and archaeological artifacts are organized around a centrally located rotunda lobby. Through their figurative forms and coloration, the galleries acquire distinct identities that complement the objects being displayed. Floor stencils, a Hornbostel tradition, are applied in the major galleries. The stencils represent architectural plans of important buildings or sites from the same culture or period as the artifacts, underscoring the didactic nature of this university museum.

The second floor contains galleries for temporary exhibitions, and university-wide facilities such as a multi-purpose reception hall and a cafe.

1

2

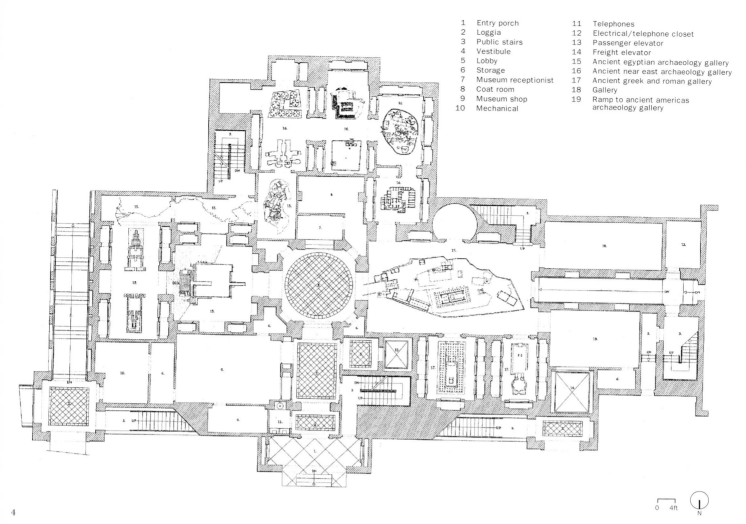

1	Entry porch	11	Telephones
2	Loggia	12	Electrical/telephone closet
3	Public stairs	13	Passenger elevator
4	Vestibule	14	Freight elevator
5	Lobby	15	Ancient egyptian archaeology gallery
6	Storage	16	Ancient near east archaeology gallery
7	Museum receptionist	17	Ancient greek and roman gallery
8	Coat room	18	Gallery
9	Museum shop	19	Ramp to ancient americas archaeology gallery
10	Mechanical		

0   4ft   N

4

6

5

Opposite:
   Ancient Egyptian Gallery
4   First floor plan
5   Museum lobby
6 & following pages:
   Ancient Classical Gallery

ASIAN ART

AFRICAN ART

9

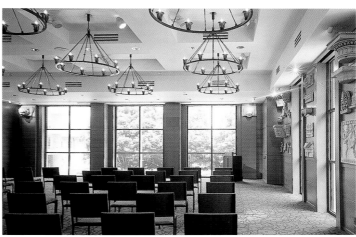

10

Opposite:
   Cafe Antica, upper floor
 9 Main lobby, upper floor
10 Reception and lecture hall, upper floor

Michael C. Carlos Museum   145

Clark County Library and Theater

Design/Completion 1990/1994
Las Vegas, Nevada
Clark County Library
120,000 square feet
Steel frame
Stucco

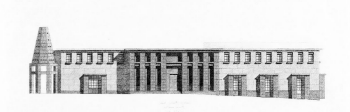

1

This project for the Flamingo Road Branch of the Clark County Library involved complete interior and exterior renovation of the original 1968 building, an addition of 27,000 square feet of library space, and a 400-seat thrust stage theater for library and community use.

The theater addition, with sculptural reliefs embedded in its main facade, is entered through a dramatic centralized structure from Flamingo Road and from an outdoor courtyard along Escondido Street. A pergola extends from its courtyard toward the rear of the site where the main entrance to the library is located. The location of the additions to the original library, and the use of porches and pergolas around the rest of the perimeter allowed the entire building to be reclad so that it reads as a single composition.

2

3

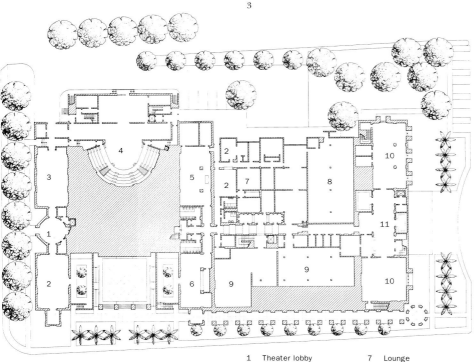

1	Theater lobby	7	Lounge
2	Reception/conference	8	Mechanical
3	Rehearsal studio	9	Periodicals storage
4	Stage	10	Periodicals reading room
5	Talking books	11	Periodicals stack
6	Computer center		

0   30   60ft   N

4

5

6

1 Library entrance facade study
2 Theater entrance court
3 Flamingo Road entrance facade
4 Lower level plan
5 Library entrance
6 Flamingo Road facade study

7

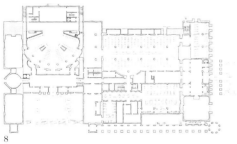

8

7   Theater with thrust stage
8   Main floor plan at entry level
9   Reader services, main level
10&11   Children's reading room, second level
12   Periodicals reading room, lower level

9

10

11

12

Denver Central Library

Design/Completion 1990/1996
Denver, Colorado
Denver Public Library
Total floor area: 133,000 square feet (renovation);
405,000 square feet (new construction)
Structural concrete waffle slabs on concrete columns
Cast stone, natural stone and copper roofing

In 1990, Graves won a design competition for the renovation and expansion of Denver's landmark library building which was designed in 1956 by the architect Burnham Hoyt. The library is sited on Civic Center Park between the city's art museum and history museum. The expansion, much greater in size than the original building, becomes a backdrop to Hoyt's composition and completes the library block south to Thirteenth Avenue. A strong new public image is established along Thirteenth Avenue facing future commercial and institutional development.

The scale and coloration of the addition, as well as the individualized massing of its various components, allow the original library to maintain its own identity as one element of a larger composition. Two major public entrances establish an east–west axis through the Great Hall, a three-story public room of urban scale which is the focal point for visitor orientation and circulation. The south-facing rotunda contains special functions such as the reference room, the periodicals center and, on the top floor, the Western History Reading Room. The latter room, which contains special collections of local materials, is centered on a timber derrick-like structure that figuratively recalls the nation's westward expansion.

1

1   South elevation study
2   View from the south
3   Acoma Plaza entrance

2

150

3

4 Detail of south facade and rotunda
5 View from the southwest
6 View from the north through Civic Center Park

4

5

6

1   Lobby
2   Great Hall
3   Circulation
4   Reference entry hall
5   Reference reading room
6   Workroom
7   Children's library
8   Children's pavilion
9   Adult fiction/popular library reading rooms
10 Stair hall
11 Library store

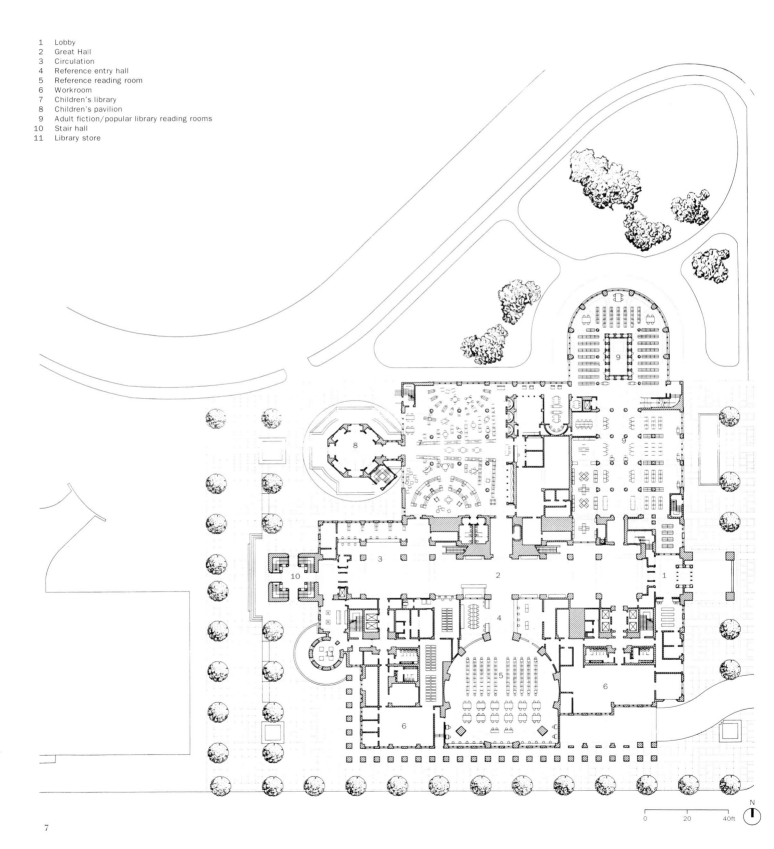

0   20   40ft

N

7

8

9

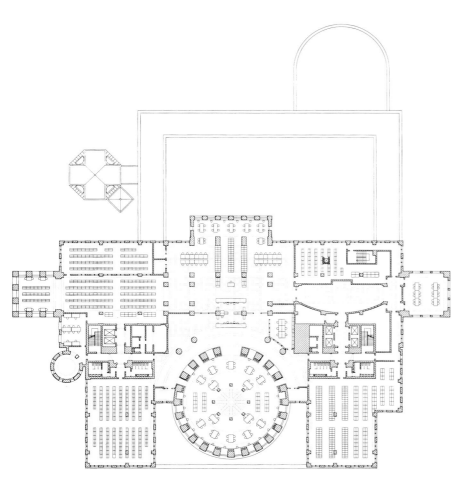

10

11

12

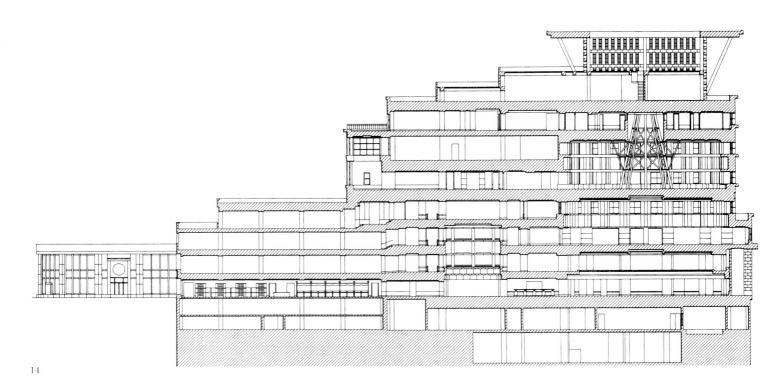

14

15

Previous pages:
Western History reading room
14   North–south section through the original building,
     the Great Hall, and the rotunda reading rooms
15   Third floor periodicals reading room
16   Children's library
17   Children's library detail
18   Children's pavilion from Acoma Plaza
19   Ground floor reference reading room
20   Library
21   Children's pavilion

16

17

18

19

20

21

Taiwan National Museum of Pre-History

Design/Completion 1993/1999
Taitung City, Taiwan
Taiwan National Museum of Pre-History
39,110 square meters
Reinforced concrete
Stucco, slate, terra cotta tile, glazed ceramic tile

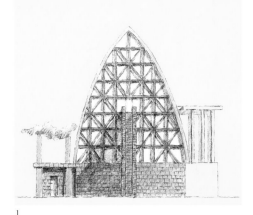

1

2

The Taiwan National Museum of Pre-History is sited near the Neolithic necropolis at Peinan, an important archaeological site. The master plan calls for a diverse group of buildings in a compound, including orientation, exhibition, and administration centers, as well as an academic and research center with faculty housing. At the center of the complex is the Court of Man, the focal point of the compound. The court's stone surface is gridded in a manner that recalls the method used by archaeologists to prepare a site for analysis. Through inscribed illustrations and text, each grid tells the story of a significant event in the natural history of Taiwan, mainland China, and the Pacific region.

Throughout the complex, the primary exterior building materials are indigenous slate, which refers to the tombstones and houses found at the archaeological site, and ceramic tile, which is typical of the region. In addition, certain building elements are made in steel using construction techniques similar to those of the vernacular wood and bamboo houses of the local Austronesian culture.

The first scheme illustrated here is Graves' competition entry for the master plan. The second scheme, a redesign of the exhibits pavilion, represents the first phase of construction.

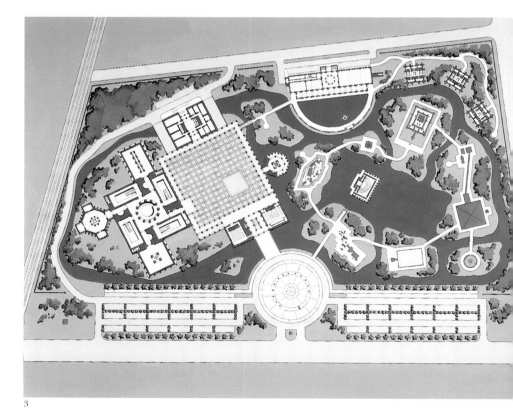

3

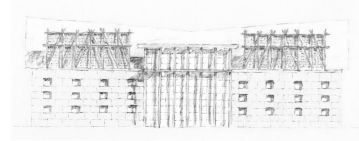

4

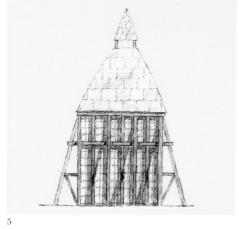

5

6

7

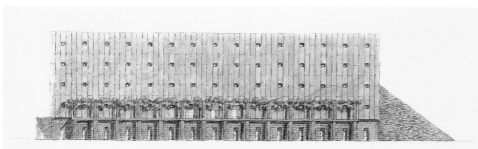

8

1   Preliminary facade study for academic center
2   Model view of competition master plan from southwest entrance
3   Competition master site plan
4   Exhibition center, south entrance pavilion
5   Preliminary facade study of dining pavilion
6   Academic center
7   Model view of exhibition center from the southwest
8   Academic center, courtyard facade

9

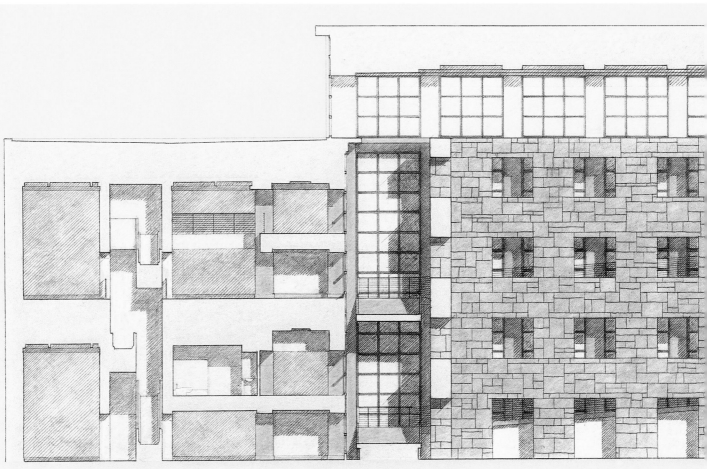

10

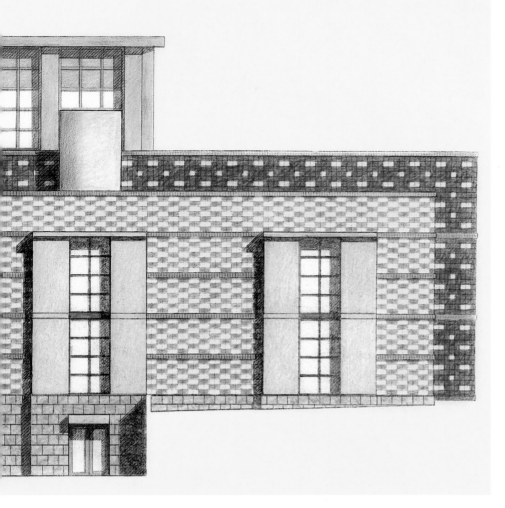

11

12

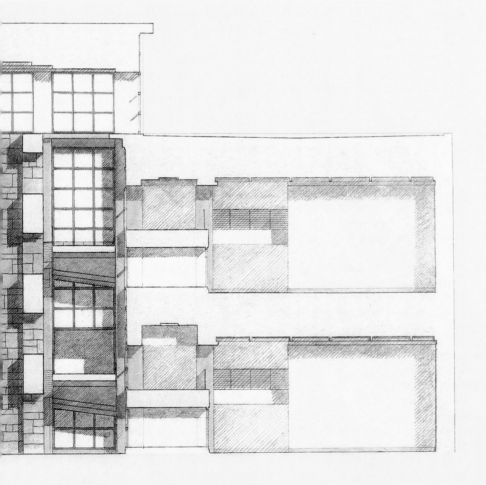

13

14

15

O'Reilly Theater

Design 1996
Pittsburgh, Pennsylvania
Pittsburgh Cultural Trust
55,000 square feet
Steel frame
Stone, brick, curtain wall, copper roof

The O'Reilly Theater is a 650-seat performance hall for the Pittsburgh Public Theater, one of the city's leading resident theater companies. The theater is one component of a mixed-use development that also includes a public park (designed in conjunction with sculptor Louise Bourgeois and landscape architect Dan Kiley) and a future office building and parking garage.

The theater auditorium has a thrust stage and horseshoe-shaped seating, providing a strong and immediate connection between audience and performer. The wood-paneled room, with curving balcony fronts profiled like architectural molding, is conceived as a fine cabinet or piece of interior furniture, furthering the impression of warmth and intimacy.

The rehearsal hall, which is the same size as the performance platform, is located above the circular entrance lobby. The curvilinear nature of the plan is restated in the vaulted roof of the rehearsal hall, reflecting the collective nature of the theater experience.

1

2

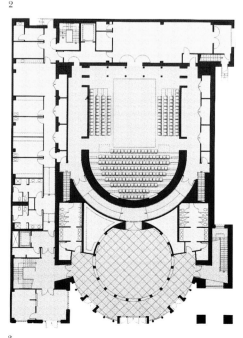

1   Site plan
2   Theater
3   First floor plan
4   Theater entrance

3   4

164

The Arts Council of Princeton

Design 1998
Princeton, New Jersey
The Arts Council of Princeton
21,240 square feet
Steel frame
Brick

1

The Arts Council of Princeton, a
community arts organization offering
programs in the visual, literary, and
performing arts, occupies a building built
in the 1930s as a WPA project. Due to the
extraordinary growth of its programs, the
Arts Council is renovating and expanding
its building to include a 200-seat theater,
a visual arts gallery, multi-purpose studios,
and a "Communiversity Room"
commemorating the relationship between
the Arts Council and Princeton University.

The expansion engages an important
street corner. The grade-level entrance
through a 12–sided lobby leads to the
theater, the gallery, and the existing
building. Above the lobby, the
Communiversity Room, with its distinctive
light monitor and expansive windows,
provides an identifiable marker at the
corner and a visual connection between
the building's activities and the
community.

2

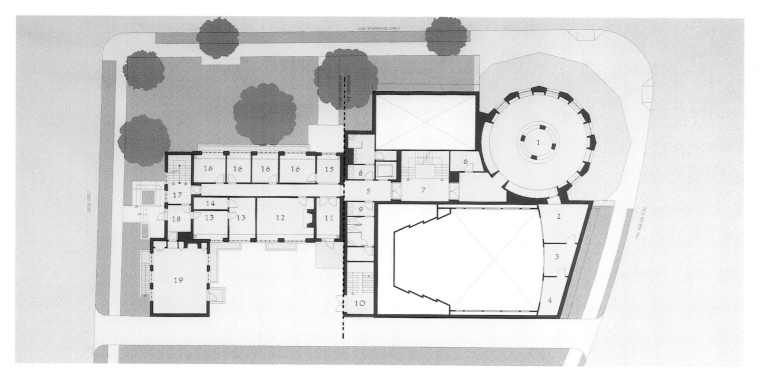

THE ARTS COUNCIL OF PRINCETON
FIRST FLOOR PLAN
SEPTEMBER 10, 1998

0   8'   16'

1. LIBRARY/COMMUNITY ROOM
2. LIGHT CONTROL
3. PROJECTION ROOM
4. SOUND CONTROL

5. ELEVATOR LOBBY
6. STORAGE
7. STAIR #1
8. MEN'S TOILET

9. WOMEN'S TOILET
10. STAIR #2
11. RECEIVING
12. ARTIST-IN-RESIDENCE STUDIO

13. CTEC OFFICE
14. CTEC STORAGE
15. RECEPTION
16. OFFICE

17. STAIR
18. VESTIBULE
19. CHILDREN'S STUDIO/
    BOOKSTORE

MICHAEL GRAVES ARCHITECT
341 NASSAU STREET, PRINCETON, NEW JERSEY 08540

3

4

5

1   View from Witherspoon Street
2   Loft Theater
3   Site and first floor plan
4   Communiversity Room
5   Theater

The Washington Monument Restoration

Design 1998
Washington, D.C.
National Park Service, Target Stores

When the Washington Monument needed major restoration work to combat years of weathering and aging, Graves was selected by a public–private partnership that involved the National Park Service and Target Stores to establish the interpretive design direction of the scaffolding that will surround the 555-foot-high monument for three years and to design the interiors of the observation and interpretive areas.

The scaffolding, engineered by the scaffolding contractor, generally follows the contours of the monument. A semi-transparent architectural fabric or mesh is attached to the scaffold system to create a "running bond" pattern simulating mortar joints; this pattern represents, at a greatly enlarged scale, the cladding of the monument which is being repointed as part of the restoration project.

By permitting views into the restoration work being performed behind the scaffolding, the design appropriately allows visitors to gain an appreciation of the importance of the task. In essence, two "monuments" are being presented to the public: the one being restored and the one erected to facilitate the restoration. The essence of the project is captured in a simple yet elegant manner without diminishing the Washington Monument's visibility or its importance as a cultural icon on the mall of the nation's capital.

1

2

3

1   Preliminary scheme, elevator cab
2   Imaginary landscape
3   Monument with scaffolding

The Washington Monument Restoration   169

Main Library of Nashville and Davidson County

Design 1998
Nashville, Tennessee
Main Library of Nashville and Davidson County
300,000 square feet
Steel frame
Stone, curtain wall, copper roof and detailing

1

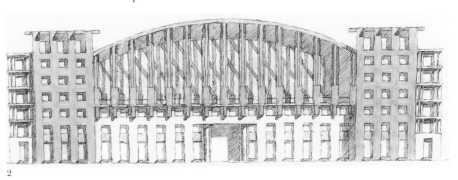

2

Graves' competition entry for Nashville's Main Library relates to its urban context, creates a dynamic and memorable public image, and provides special places for individual study and contemplation. The library, placed at the northernmost edge of the site, maintains the streetwall of Church Street, one of Nashville's most significant thoroughfares. The massing and entrance are organized symmetrically about the axis of Capitol Boulevard, which becomes an urban forecourt to the building, leading up to William Strickland's prominent Tennessee State Capitol. The building's vaulted copper roof emphasizes the collective nature of the institution, while the upper level colonnade of the Grand Reading Room frames individual views to the Capitol.

Internally, the library is organized around two large public spaces stacked above each other: the main lobby and the Grand Reading Room. In the lobby, information and circulation desks are immediately visible as are upper level activities, particularly the Children's Department on the second floor. A portion of the south-facing garage roof adjacent to the library is developed as a garden within which is located a whimsical children's pavilion for story-telling and other events.

The Grand Reading Room for the adult collections, located on the fourth and fifth floors, is organized around a two-story vaulted atrium surrounded by wooden columns and struts. These, along with the warm wood detailing and paneling throughout the library, are reminiscent of the lore of this hilly, forested area of Tennessee and enhance the public's identification with the region's collective memory.

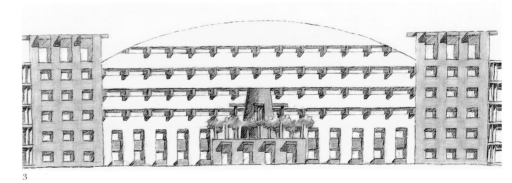

3

4

170

5

6

1 Massing study
2 Church Street elevation
3 South elevation
4 Church Street entrance
5 Main lobby
6 Grand Reading Room

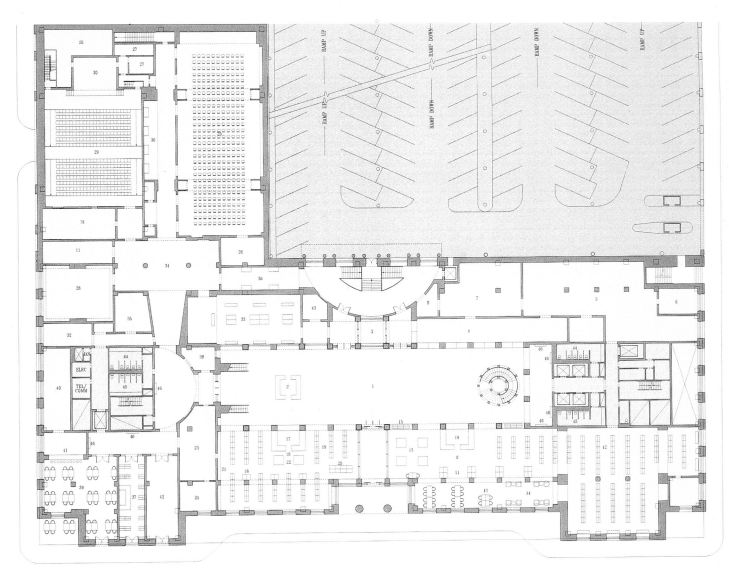

CHURCH STREET

LEGEND

1. ENTRANCE LOBBY

2. INFORMATION COUNTER
3. BUILDING SECURITY

4. CIRCULATION SERVICE DESK

5. CIRCULATION WORK ROOM
6. SUPERVISOR'S OFFICE
7. SORTING ROOM
8. BOOK RETURN

9. POPULAR MATERIALS AND ADULT FICTION

10. SERVICE DESK
11. OPAC STATIONS
12. DISPLAY & FICTION SHELVING
13. READING
14. LOUNGE SEATING
15. DISPLAY

16. AUDIOVISUAL SERVICES

17. SERVICE COUNTER
18. OPAC STATIONS
19. AV SHELVING
20. LISTENING AND VIEWING STATIONS
21. BENCH SEATING
22. DISPLAY
23. AUDIOVISUAL SERVICES WORK ROOM
24. SUPERVISOR'S OFFICE

CONFERENCE CENTER

25. MULTI-PURPOSE MEETING ROOM
26. STORAGE
27. GREEN ROOM
28. CONFERENCE ROOM
29. AUDITORIUM
30. STAGE
31. BUILDING-WIDE PROJECTION ROOM
32. CATERING KITCHEN
33. GALLERY
34. PRE-FUNCTION ROOM
35. GALLERY STORAGE
36. GALLERY DISPLAY

ENTERPRISE SPACES

37. BOOKSTORE
38. GIFT SHOP
39. CAFE
40. CAFE KITCHEN
41. CAFE COUNTER

42. PRINTING SERVICE
43. FRIEND'S OFFICE

44. WOMEN'S RESTROOM
45. MEN'S RESTROOM
46. ART

"Rome Reborn" Exhibition

Design/Completion 1992/1993
Washington, D.C.
Library of Congress
5,800 square feet
Wood
Wood, fabric

"Rome Reborn: The Vatican Library and Renaissance Culture" was the inaugural exhibition held in the remodeled southwest wing of the Library of Congress. The exhibition featured a notable selection of manuscripts from the Vatican Library. As this was the first in a series of exhibitions, the casework was designed to adapt to a variety of installations and conservation requirements. Two types of cases were designed—a tall, column-like case and a low, wall-like case—which can be arranged singly, in pairs, and in groups.

Because of the unique program and the spatial character of this wing of the building, the exhibit was organized in seven bays, in keeping with the architecture of the room. Instead of "constructing" the exhibit in the room, Graves "furnished" the rooms with the cases in a rhythm reminiscent of a city street. The cases were thus treated like large-scale furniture or small buildings and given an architectural character complementary to the scale and classical style of the spaces they occupy.

1   Display case
2   Entrance signage

3

4

5

6

7

3   Exhibit entrance
4   Typical display case in pavilion
5&6 Exhibit in Southwest Curtain
7   "Archaeology" display cases

Universities

Bryan Hall

Design/Completion 1987/1995
Charlottesville, Virginia
University of Virginia
40,000 square feet
Steel frame
Brick, metal roof, wood trim

1

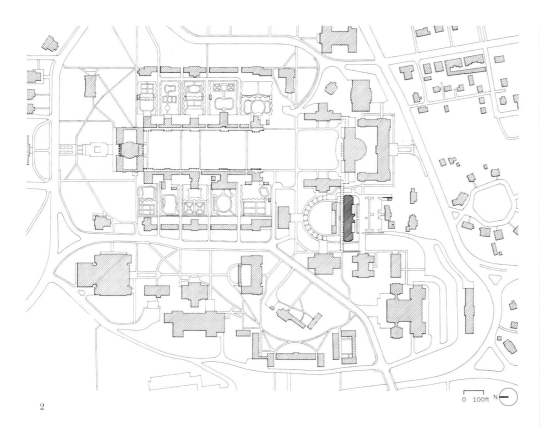

2

3

4

Bryan Hall is a 40,000-square-foot classroom and office building located in the university's South Central Grounds near the historic structures of the original "academical village" designed by Thomas Jefferson. It is also adjacent to Fiske Kimball's McIntire Amphitheater and Stanford White's Cabell Hall. The materials, scale, and fenestration of Bryan Hall are similar to those of buildings in the immediate context without replicating them directly.

The site for Bryan Hall is relatively flat but to either side the ground rises steeply to

landscaped or masonry terraces. To improve pedestrian circulation in this section of the campus and to connect this building to neighboring academic facilities, the project includes an elevated pedestrian bridge at the third level. The bridge is designed as a covered peristyle that, without imitating the buildings on Thomas Jefferson's Lawn, has a similar sense of rhythm and repetition. The bridge also acts as a backdrop to the amphitheater stage, providing a sense of closure to that space.

5

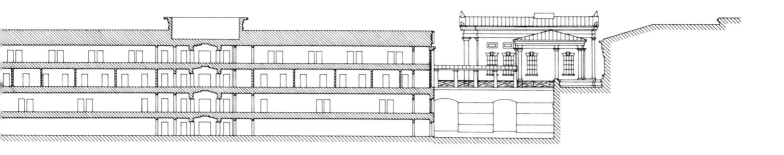

1   East–west section
2   Site plan
3   South elevation
4   View of building and bridge across
     McIntire Amphitheater
5   South facade

Bryan Hall   179

1 Entry hall
2 Office
3 Staff
4 Classroom
5 Laboratory
6 Pedestrian bridge
7 Porch
8 Existing stage

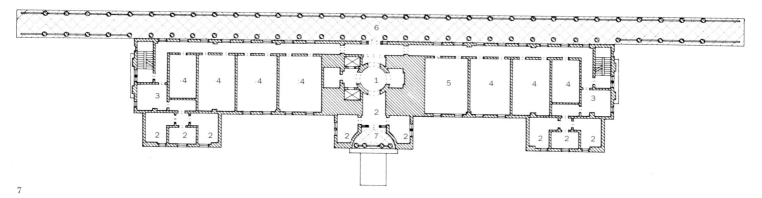

7

9

Opposite:
  Entrance detail
7 Bridge level plan
8 Pedestrian bridge looking west
9 Rotunda on bridge level looking toward Garett Hall

8

Institute for Theoretical Physics

Design/Completion 1990/1994
Santa Barbara, California
University of California at Santa Barbara
27,000 square feet
Type 5 wood frame
Stucco, wood, clay tile

The Institute for Theoretical Physics forms the eastern gateway to the Santa Barbara campus, adjacent to the engineering complex, and is situated on a bluff overlooking the Pacific Ocean. The irregular configuration of the site and the desire to orient the building to both the ocean and the engineering buildings produced a plan organized in two office wings parallel to these site elements.

A cylindrical pavilion housing the library connects the two wings at one end of the building. The space between the wings is developed as a landscaped courtyard, reached through the building's common room.

The building's articulation, materials, and coloration reflect the indigenous architecture of the region and the original campus. The copper awnings and wooden trellises with climbing vines help control the intensity of the sun.

Opposite:
 View from the east

2

2   Lagoon Road facade
3   Pergola in courtyard
Opposite:
   View from pergola

3

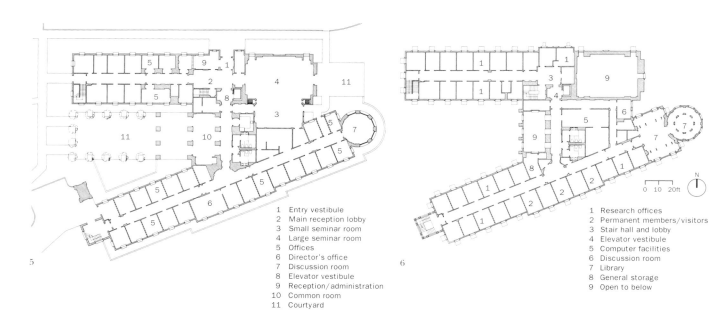

5

6

1 Entry vestibule
2 Main reception lobby
3 Small seminar room
4 Large seminar room
5 Offices
6 Director's office
7 Discussion room
8 Elevator vestibule
9 Reception/administration
10 Common room
11 Courtyard

1 Research offices
2 Permanent members/visitors
3 Stair hall and lobby
4 Elevator vestibule
5 Computer facilities
6 Discussion room
7 Library
8 General storage
9 Open to below

7

8

5 Ground floor plan
6 Second floor plan
7 Library table and lamps
8 Common room
9 Library

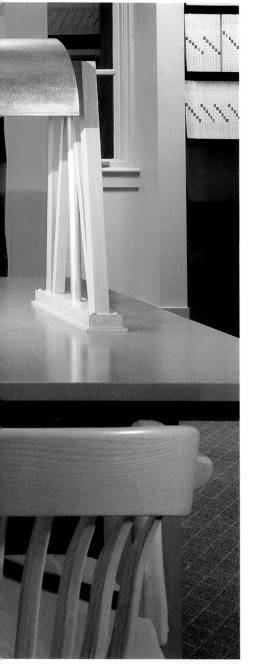

9

Engineering Research Center

Design/Completion 1990/1995
Cincinnati, Ohio
University of Cincinnati
167,200 square feet
Steel frame
Brick, cast stone, copper roof

The Engineering Research Center terminates the axis of University Avenue, the main approach to the university campus from the east, and connects to Rhodes Hall, another engineering building located higher up the steeply sloping site. The Center is organized as a series of equal six-story bays or pavilions. Projecting from the body of the building, the entrance pavilion contains faculty offices and conference rooms above an open loggia at the plaza level. Exterior and interior public stairs accommodate the 17-foot change in grade from the building entrance to the plaza level.

The organization of the building provides flexible laboratories and technical spaces at the center, and offices and classrooms around the perimeter. The exterior materials of terra cotta and ochre brick with cast stone details are consistent with the older sections of the campus. The vaulted roof, dormer windows, and stacks are sheathed in copper.

1 Copper roof detail
2 View of entrance facade from the east
3 Entrance elevation study
4 View from the northwest
5 East–west section through loggia, lobby, and Rhodes Hall bridge
6 View of facade from the south
7 Ground floor plan
Following page:
    Second level of entrance stair hall

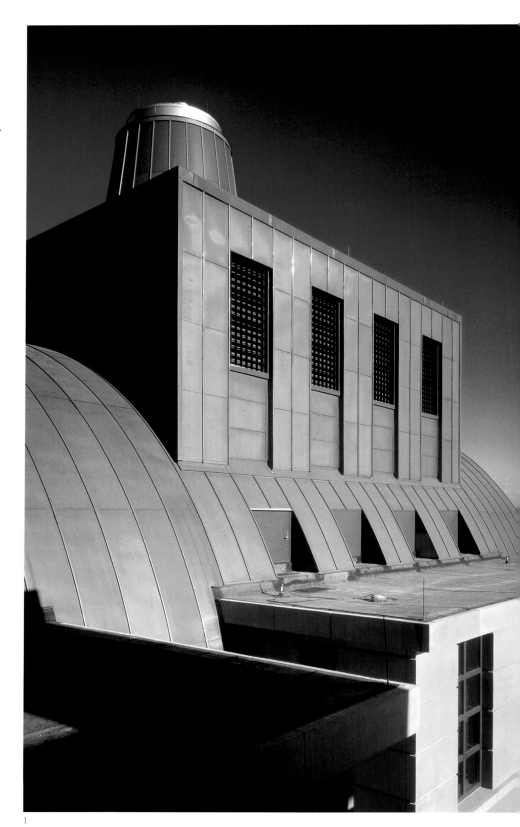

1

2

3

4

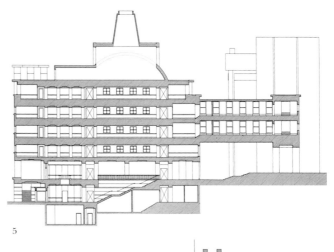

5

6

7

1	Lobby	6	Lounge
2	Loggia	7	Mechanical shaft
3	Seminar room	8	Laboratory
4	Lecture hall lobby	9	Student office
5	Lecture hall	10	Faculty office

0   30ft

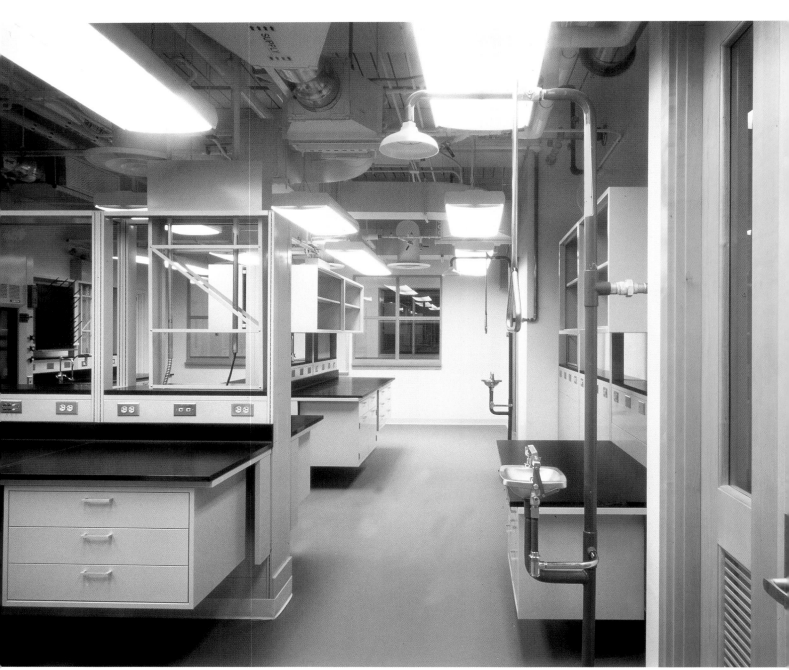

9

10

9   Laboratory
10 Lecture hall

Saint Martin's College Library

Design 1995
Lacey, Washington
Saint Martin's College
40,000 square feet
Steel frame
Brick

1

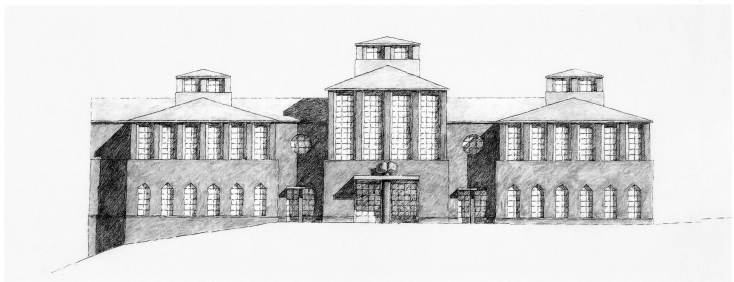

2

Saint Martin's College is a Benedictine institution that serves students living on campus as well as those commuting from the surrounding area. The library, which will house the college collections and provide instructional space, is central to the educational program and the students' individual academic pursuits while on campus. The site, located in a developing area of the campus, slopes steeply down from existing academic buildings toward the entrance road and thus offers the possibility of establishing a new, visible academic core distinct from the more private monastic zone of the other side of the campus.

The building is organized around a central core of stacks and collection areas, lit from above by clerestories. Reading and study areas around the perimeter of the building provide natural light and views of the surrounding forest. References to Saint Martin's Benedictine traditions are made through the use of pointed arch windows and other detailing and through the respect shown for the natural environment surrounding the library.

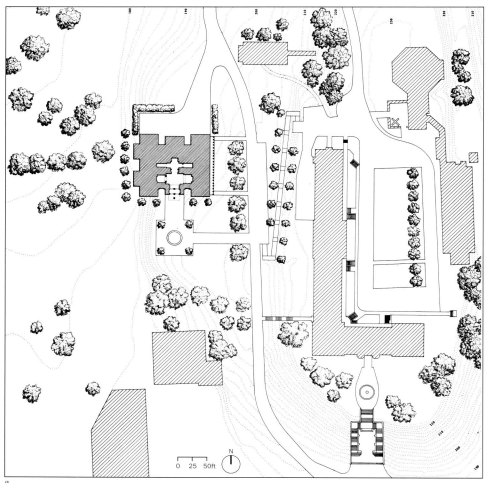

3

194

4

5

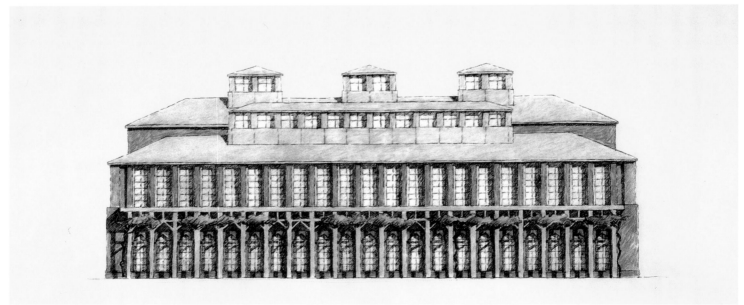

6

7

8

1 Lobby
2 Public catalog
3 Circulation desk
4 Reference
5 Periodicals
6 Administrative offices
7 Technical services
8 Shipping/receiving/storage
9 Staff room

5 West elevation
6 East elevation
7 Model view from the south
8 Second floor plan

Laurel Hall Student Residence

Design/Completion 1995/1997
Newark, New Jersey
New Jersey Institute of Technology
85,000 square feet
Bearing wall construction, block and concrete plank

Laurel Hall, a 300-bed student residence, forms the longitudinal boundary of a new campus green that features an existing residential hall at one end and a site for future development at the other. The program required a mixture of single and double rooms, which have been arranged in three different suite configurations. The ground floor contains various common facilities such as recreation and meeting rooms, study lounges, a television lounge, and an apartment for the resident advisor. The upper floors include a study lounge at each end of the central corridor.

On the exterior, the centralized entrance portico acts as a base for a symbolic front porch consisting of 16 four-story painted aluminum columns supporting a thin flat roof. In order to lend a more residential scale to the building's 250-foot-long facade, the single rooms and stairs are recessed from the main facade and finished with a dark gray-blue stucco as if in deep shadow. Projecting cast stone sills, window surrounds, and cornices also create shadows that serve to enliven the building and make it inviting for its student population.

1

1   Entrance facade
2   East elevation study
3   Entrance portico
4   View from the northwest

2

3

4

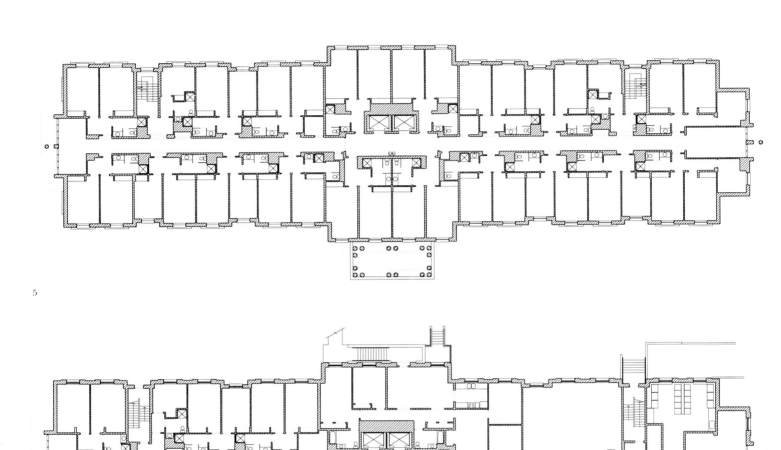

5

6

7

8

5   Typical floor plan
6   Ground floor plan
7   Lobby
8   Lounge

Residential

Portside Apartment Tower

Design/Completion 1988/1991
Yokohama, Japan
Housing and Urban Development Commission
235,000 square feet
Reinforced concrete
Glazed tile, painted concrete

Graves was commissioned to design this 27-story apartment tower for Yokohama's Portside District D, an area called Minato Mirai 21 ("waterfront for the 21st century"). The district consists of mixed-use development on a landfill on Yokohama Bay. This apartment tower and an adjacent office building of similar scale are the most significant buildings in the development.

The building is organized as a tripartite composition in which the base, middle, and top appear as discrete elements. The base of the building, intended primarily for public use, contains retail shops and galleries. The tower above is divided into two sections, and distinctive fenestration and balconies allow the residents a choice of apartment types. Continuous balconies are required on all levels of the building to meet local fire exit codes.

The distinctive top of the building is developed as two-story penthouse apartments.

1

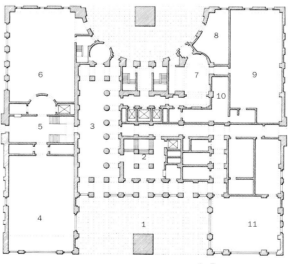

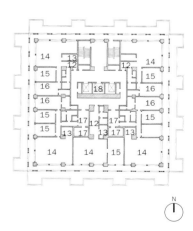

1	Terrace	
2	Lobby	
3	Atrium	
4	Temporary exhibition	
5	Gallery lobby	
6	Gallery store	
7	Residential lobby	
8	Retail	
9	Bicycles	
10	Concierge	
11	Restaurant	

12	Entry hall
13	Kitchen
14	Living/dining room
15	Bedroom
16	Master bedroom
17	Service
18	Lobby

1 View from the bay
2 Ground floor plan
3 Apartment plans, 17th to 26th floors
4 View from the mainland

2

3

204

Momochi District Apartment Building

Design/Completion 1988/1989
Fukuoka, Japan
Fukuoka Jisho Co., Ltd.
40,000 square feet (total area)
Reinforced concrete
Red Barouli sandstone

1

For the 1989 Asian–Pacific Exposition, the Japanese city of Fukuoka reclaimed 193 acres of its waterfront for a model city. Several pairs of architects were assigned to design five-story apartment buildings. The program for the apartment buildings was ground-level retail shops and four upper stories containing 10 apartments with a mix of one to four bedrooms.

Graves was assigned the corner site at the main highway entrance to the exposition. The placement of the building on the site was determined by strict requirements for setbacks and massing. The ground level is linked by retail shops and restaurants to the companion apartment building designed by Chicago architect Stanley Tigerman.

2

3

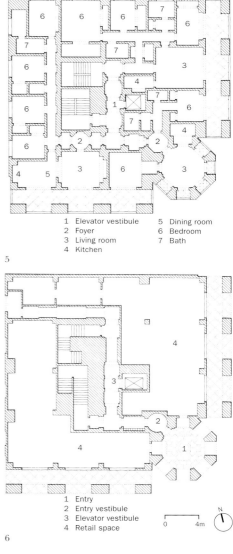

1 Elevator vestibule   5 Dining room
2 Foyer   6 Bedroom
3 Living room   7 Bath
4 Kitchen

5

1 Entry
2 Entry vestibule
3 Elevator vestibule
4 Retail space

0   4m   N

6

4

1 View from the southeast
2 Detail of southeast corner tower
3 View from the southeast
4 Model apartment living room with "Kyoto"
   furniture collection
5 Second and third floor plans
6 Ground floor plan

Nexus Momochi Residential Tower

Design/Completion 1993/1996
Fukuoka, Japan
Fukuoka Jisho Co., Ltd., Maeda Corporation
275,000 square feet
Steel, reinforced concrete
Precast concrete, glass curtain wall

This 27-story luxury apartment tower is located on the bay in Fukuoka, at the end of the axis established by Graves' Momochi District apartment building. The tower, the tallest building in the internationally acclaimed Nexus residential district, occupies one of the most prestigious sites in this development.

The building's exterior consists of a slender, ochre precast concrete frame applied over a glass curtain wall. The transparent quality of this framing system gives the tower a luminous presence when seen from the water, making it appear as an abstract version of a lighthouse. The facade's generous fenestration also provides the apartments with spectacular waterfront views. Graves designed six penthouse apartments in addition to the exterior and the public spaces of the building.

Opposite:
  View from the southwest
2   Pergola
3   Reception
4   Ground floor plan
5   Typical floor plan, 13th to 19th floor

208

2

3

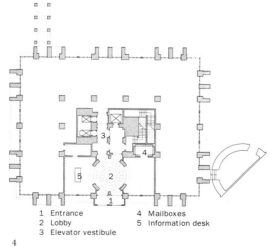

4

1 Entrance   4 Mailboxes
2 Lobby   5 Information desk
3 Elevator vestibule

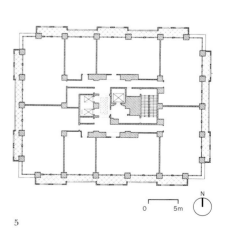

5

0   5m   N

1500 Ocean Drive and Ocean Steps

Design/Completion 1994/1999
Miami Beach, Florida
Jefferson Plaza, Ltd.
475,000 square feet
Reinforced concrete
Stucco

1

2

The residential condominiums at 1500 Ocean Drive and their companion retail center, Ocean Steps, are located at the terminus of Ocean Drive in the South Beach section of Miami Beach, Florida. The project is adjacent to the city's famous Art Deco district and incorporates the historic Bancroft Hotel.

The organization of the project's components respects the scale and character of the surrounding neighborhoods. The building's forms, colors, and details reflect the oceanfront location as well as local building traditions. The condominium building is oriented toward the beach, providing the rooms of its cylindrical towers with panoramic views.

3

1　Site and ground floor plan
2　Competition phase: ocean facade
3　Competition phase: Fifteenth Street facade
　　of residential building; Bancroft building on left

4   Residential building model: view from ocean
5   Residential building: typical floor plan

4

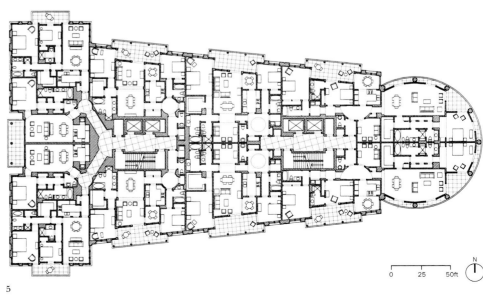

0   25   50ft

5

6

6   Model: Fifteenth Street facade; Bancroft building
and commercial development on left; residential
building on right

Beach House

Design/Completion 1990/1992
Malibu, California
6,000 square feet
Wood frame
Alaskan cedar

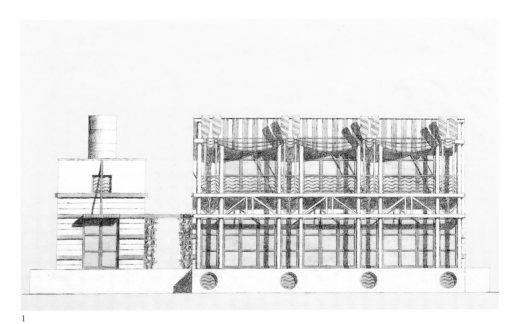

1

2

The street face of this residence on the Pacific Ocean coastline is rather solid in order to screen out automobile noise and provide privacy. In contrast, the ocean side is opened as a large framed porch to take advantage of the view and the ocean breezes. Adjacent to the house is a small structure housing a screening room. This building is covered in lattice designed to support climbing vines. The interiors are open and airy, consistent with the casual nature of summertime and weekend use.

3

1 Preliminary oceanfront elevation
2 Ocean terrace detail
3 Ocean facade
Opposite:
    Screening room pavilion

216

6

5   Screening room pavilion
6   West facade of living room

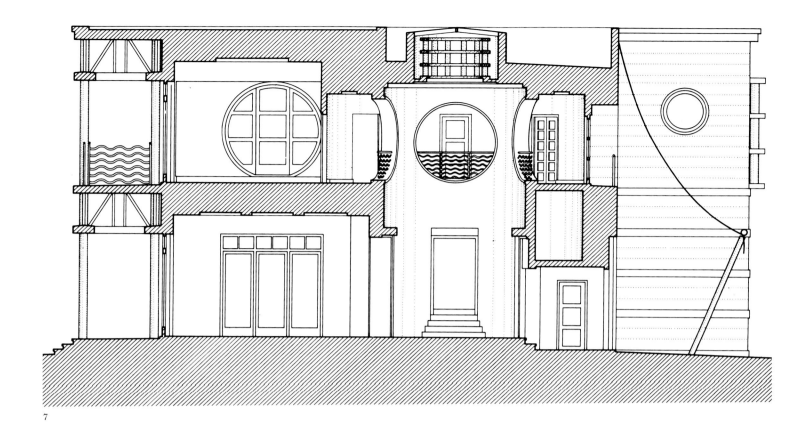

7

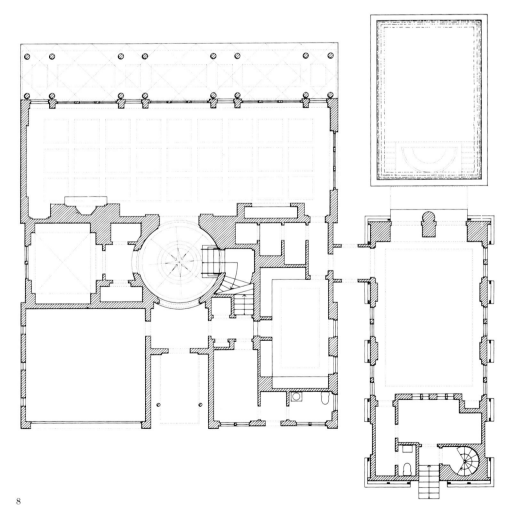

7 Section through living room and entry rotunda   8

8 Ground floor plan

Opposite:
    Central rotunda

10

11

10   Living room
11   Dining room
Opposite:
    Master bedroom terrace

LIFE Magazine Dream House

Design 1996
LIFE Magazine
2,100 square feet

Michael Graves was commissioned by
LIFE Magazine to design its third annual
prototypical "dream house." *LIFE*'s goal
was to show the readers that a well-known
architect could create a house design
comparable in size and cost to the average
new house being built in the United
States. The design anticipates flexibility
in its plans and materials in order to be
adaptable to the requirements of various
families and sites.

The rotunda foyer is central to the
organization of the plan and sets up
the procession through the house. The
orderly nature of the architecture and
interiors allows the users to achieve a
comfortable sense of well-being in the
house and yet be able to personalize
it for their individual lifestyles.

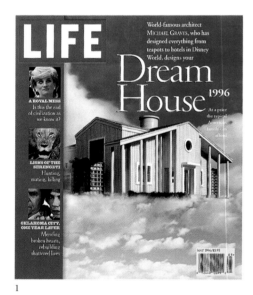

1

1   May 1996 *LIFE* cover
2   View from street

2

3

4

5

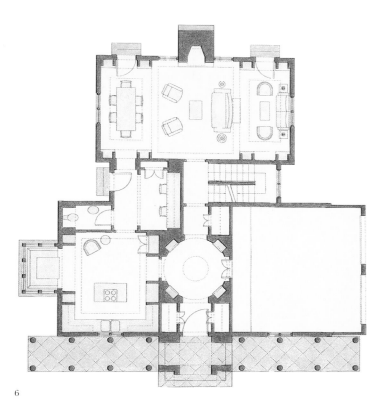

6

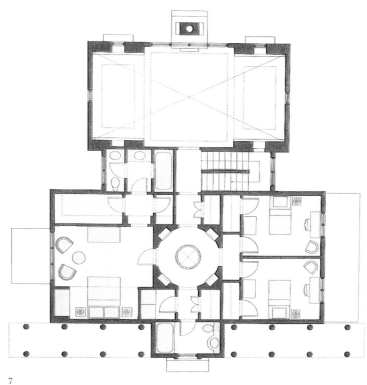

7

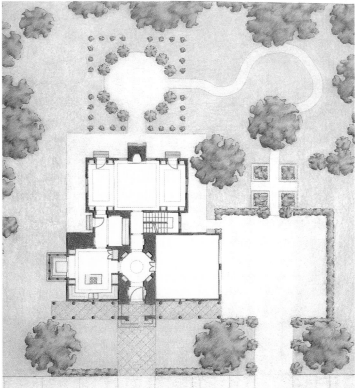

8

3   Street elevation
4   Living room interior
5   Kitchen
6   First floor plan
7   Second floor plan
8   Site plan

Graves Residence: The Warehouse

Design/Completion 1974/1992
Princeton, New Jersey
Michael Graves
6,000 gross square feet (approx.)
Masonry bearing wall
Stucco on masonry, oak and concrete flooring

Michael Graves' residence is a converted warehouse built in 1926 by Italian stonemasons who were constructing various buildings at Princeton University at that time. It was built in a typical Tuscan vernacular style using hollow clay tile, brick, and stucco. The L-shaped building was originally divided into many storage cells and has been renovated in stages. The north wing, completed in 1987, is entered through an outdoor courtyard that was once a truck dock. It includes a living room, dining room, and library with a garden terrace on the first floor and a master bedroom and study on the second floor. The subsequent renovation of the west wing contains the kitchen and extensive guest quarters.

The use of daylight throughout the house deliberately reinforces the context of particular rooms and suggests a continuity between the building and the surrounding natural landscape. Rather than flooding the house with diffuse light characteristic of the outdoors, Graves' more selective approach energizes the interiors with a dynamic sense of the time of day and year.

The house is carefully furnished with an extensive collection of books, objects, furniture, and art, creating convivial settings that convey a sense of habitation and reinforce a feeling of domesticity.

1

2

228

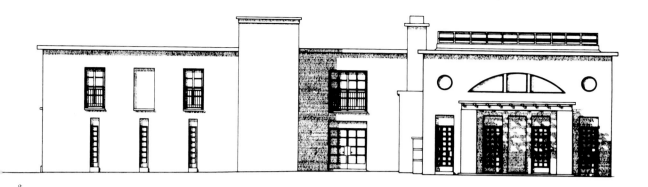

3

4

5

1 View from east garden
2 Espaliered roses on west wing courtyard facade
3 East elevation
4 View from the street
5 North facade detail

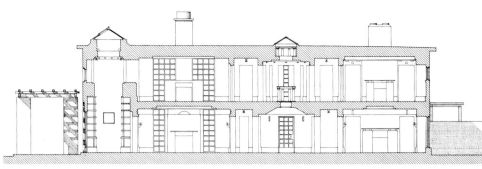

7

8

Opposite:
  Living room
7 East–west section through north wing
8 Library

9

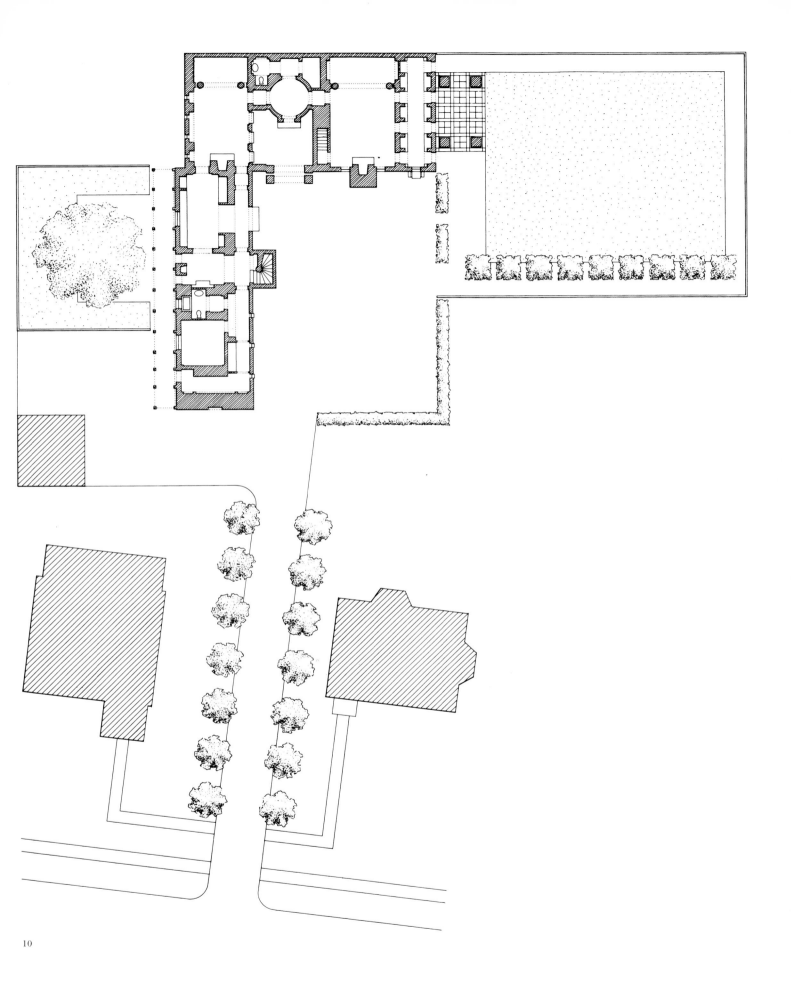

10

9   Dining room
10   Site plan

11

12

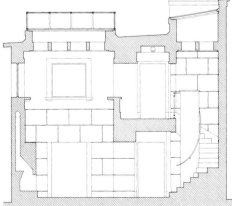

13

11 Kitchen looking toward breakfast room
12 Breakfast room looking toward west garden
13 West wing: north–south section through breakfast room and stair

Firm Profile

Biographies

Michael Graves, FAIA
Principal

American architect Michael Graves has been at the forefront of architectural and interior design since he began his practice in Princeton, New Jersey, in 1964. Now the Schirmer Professor of Architecture at Princeton University, where he has taught since 1962, Graves is an influential theorist as well as a diversified and prolific designer. Since the early 1980s, his work has directly influenced the transformation of urban architecture from the abstractions of commercial Modernism toward more contextual responses. Critic Paul Goldberger, writing in *The New York Times*, has said that "Graves … is truly the most original voice American architecture has produced in some time."

Working closely with the other Principals of his firm, Michael Graves & Associates, Graves himself is personally involved at all levels of design activity, originating and drawing projects and providing ongoing criticism and direction to the staff. The 75-person firm, with offices in Princeton, New Jersey, and New York City, has a highly diverse international practice in architecture, interior design, product design, and graphic design. The architectural practice, as illustrated in this monograph, encompasses a wide variety of building types including large-scale mixed-use projects; office buildings and corporate headquarters; university buildings of many types; civic institutions such as courthouses and governmental office buildings; public educational and cultural facilities such as libraries, museums, and theaters; hotels and resorts; facilities for sports, entertainment, and retail enterprises; apartment buildings and single-family residences. Over 100 awards and citations have been awarded to Michael Graves and the firm, including 10 National Honor Awards and over 50 state awards from the American Institute of Architects.

Graves is well-known for interior design and custom-designed furnishings as well as for his extensive consumer products design practice, which features products for manufacturers such as Alessi, Baldinger, Duravit, Valli & Valli, and Steuben, as well as lines of furnishings, housewares, and decorative accessories for the American retailer Target.

A native of Indianapolis, Indiana, Michael Graves received his architectural training at the University of Cincinnati and Harvard University. In 1960 he won the Rome Prize and studied for two years at the American Academy in Rome, of which he is presently a Trustee. He is a Fellow of the American Institute of Architects and a member of the Academy of Arts and Letters.

Patrick J. Burke, AIA
Principal

Since joining the firm in 1982, Patrick Burke has been involved with a wide variety of projects, especially in the hospitality and retail fields. He was the Project Architect for the Walt Disney World Resort Dolphin and Swan Hotels in Orlando, Florida; the Hotel New York at EuroDisneyland Park near Paris, France; the Astrid Plaza Hotel in Antwerp, Belgium; and six hotels and related facilities in Egypt, including the award-winning Miramar Resort Hotel on the Red Sea in El Gouna. Other work includes numerous private residences as well as institutional projects such as the award-winning renovation and subsequent expansion of the Michael C. Carlos Museum at Emory University in Atlanta, the Historical Center for Industry and Labor in Youngstown, Ohio, and Saint Martin's College in Lacey, Washington.

Most of Patrick Burke's projects require extensive interior design, including custom-designed furniture and furnishings, graphics, and artwork, and he is therefore highly involved with the firm's interior design and consumer products departments. He was the designer for the 1993 exhibition "The Birth of Democracy" held at the National Archives. He was also co-editor of two monographs on the work of Michael Graves. Patrick Burke received a Bachelor of Architecture from the University of Illinois, Chicago Circle, and a Master of Architecture from Princeton University.

John Diebboll, AIA
Principal

John Diebboll is the Principal in charge of Michael Graves & Associates' New York City office. A member of the firm since 1984, he has participated in the design and management of a wide variety of institutional projects, including public libraries in Denver, Colorado, Topeka, Kansas, Alexandria, Virginia, and Las Vegas, Nevada, as well as a library for the French Institute/ Alliance Française in New York City; facilities for the arts such as the Indianapolis Art Center and the award-winning National Museum of Pre-History in Taiwan; and educational facilities for several preparatory schools and colleges.

He has also overseen the design of a wide variety of residential projects, including the Miami Beach condominium building, 1500 Ocean Drive, and single-family residences in New York, Connecticut, Ohio, New Jersey, and Amsterdam, as well as commercial projects in the United States and Asia.

John Diebboll received a Bachelor of Arts from Bennington College and a Master of Architecture from Princeton University.

Susan Howard, Esq.
Principal

Susan Howard has been advising Michael Graves & Associates on financial and legal matters since 1987. She has shaped the firm's approach to contracts and has played a key role in developing its business plan. Recently, she has focused her attention on the diversification of the practice and on the development of the interiors and consumer products departments. She received a Bachelor of Science degree from Beaver College, her Law degree from Seton Hall, and an L.L.M. in Taxation from New York University.

Gary Lapera, AIA
Principal

Gary Lapera has managed the design of many of the firm's residential projects, while also directing large mixed-use projects in Europe, the Middle East, and Asia. He has been in charge of two residential towers and an office building in Fukuoka, Japan; a residential and mixed-use building in Seoul, Korea; and the Fujian Xingye Banking Tower project in Shanghai, China. Completed office buildings include the award-winning Thomson Consumer Electronics Americas Headquarters in Indianapolis, Indiana, and Castalia, the headquarters for the Ministry of Health, Welfare and Sport in The Hague. He has also worked on several sports and recreational projects in the United States and Asia, including sports training centers and golf clubs.

Gary Lapera received his education at Cornell University and Harvard University.

Karen Nichols, AIA
Principal

Since 1977, Karen Nichols has had responsibility for managing Michael Graves & Associates' architectural practice and for overseeing the start-up and ongoing operation of its consumer products division. As an architect, she has managed numerous complex projects and has produced master plans and building programs, particularly for artistic and educational institutions. She has been the Principal in charge of the renovation and expansion of The Newark Museum since 1982 and The Detroit Institute of Arts since 1988, both of which have involved phased construction. Other projects include the Fargo-Moorhead Cultural Bridge, the Riverbend Music Center in Cincinnati, the preplanning study for Bryan Hall at the University of Virginia, and a master plan for the New Jersey Institute of Technology.

Karen Nichols has been the co-editor of three monographs on the work of Michael Graves and has designed and managed over 100 exhibitions of the firm's work. She received a Bachelor of Arts from Smith College and a Master of Architecture from Massachusetts Institute of Technology.

Thomas P. Rowe, AIA
Principal

Since joining Michael Graves & Associates in 1984, Thomas Rowe has been in charge of many of the firm's largest and most complex projects, including numerous mixed-use and institutional buildings in the United States and Asia. Representative projects include the Denver Central Library, the O'Reilly Theater in Pittsburgh, the NCAA 2000 Headquarters and Hall of Champions in Indianapolis, the Engineering Research Center at the University of Cincinnati, the Hyatt Regency Hotel and Office Building in Fukuoka, Japan, and the design competition for the Singapore National Library. Prominent projects in Washington, D.C. include the World Bank's International Finance Corporation Headquarters and the United States Courthouse renovation and expansion, both located on Pennsylvania Avenue, as well as the scaffolding and interior renovation of the Washington Monument.

Prior to joining MGA, Thomas Rowe worked for the Graves-Warnecke Joint Venture on the Humana Building in Louisville, Kentucky. He received his education at Catholic University in Washington, D.C. and at Princeton University.

Awards

National Honor Award
American Institute of Architects
Denver Central Library Interiors
Denver, Colorado
1998

Architectural Projects Honor Award
American Institute of Architects, New Jersey
Chapter
Delaware River Port Authority
Camden, New Jersey
1998

Good Design Award
The Chicago Athenaeum
Toaster (in partnership with Black & Decker)

New Jersey Golden Trowel Award
International Masonry Institute
Laurel Hall, New Jersey Institute of Technology
Newark, New Jersey
1998

Steve Dach Architectural Excellence Award
Rocky Mountain Masonry Institute
Denver Central Library
Denver, Colorado
1998

William Howard Taft Award
University of Cincinnati Alumni Association
1998

Architectural Projects Honor Award
American Institute of Architects, New Jersey
Chapter
International Finance Corporation
Washington, D.C.
1997

Excellence in Construction Award
Associated Builders and Contractors
International Finance Corporation
Washington, D.C.
1997

GQ **Magazine Man of the Year**
1997

Marble Architectural Awards
Internazionale Marmi e Macchine Carrara
Denver Central Library
Denver, Colorado
1997

10th Annual Urban Beautification Award
Nexus Momochi Residential Tower
Fukuoka, Japan
1997

Interior Architecture Award
American Institute of Architects, New York
Chapter
Michael C. Carlos Museum
Emory University, Atlanta, Georgia
1996

33rd Annual Concrete Awards Merit Award
NJ Chapter of American Concrete Institute
and NJ Concrete and Aggregate Association
Archdiocesan Center
Newark, New Jersey
1996

Architectural Projects Honor Award
American Institute of Architects, New Jersey
Chapter
Miramar Resort Hotel
El Gouna, Egypt
1996

Architectural Projects Honor Award
American Institute of Architects, New Jersey
Chapter
National Bank of Abu Dhabi
Abu Dhabi, United Arab Emirates
1996

36th Annual Building Contractor's Society Award
Fukuoka Hyatt Regency Hotel and Office
Building
Fukuoka, Japan
1995

Architectural Projects Honor Award
American Institute of Architects, New Jersey
Chapter
Denver Central Library
Denver, Colorado
1995

Architectural Projects Honor Award
American Institute of Architects, New Jersey
Chapter
Kasumi Research and Training Center
Tsukuba City, Japan
1995

Eighth Annual Fukuoka Urban Beautification Award
Fukuoka Hyatt Regency Hotel and Office
Building
Fukuoka, Japan
1995

Honor Award
American Institute of Architects, Cincinnati
Chapter
Engineering Research Center
University of Cincinnati
Cincinnati, Ohio
1995

The Collab Award for Excellence in Design
The Philadelphia Museum of Art
1995

Architectural Projects Honor Award
American Institute of Architects, New Jersey
Chapter
Michael C. Carlos Museum
Emory University, Atlanta, Georgia
1994

Architectural Projects Honor Award
American Institute of Architects, New Jersey
Chapter
Thomson Consumer Electronics Americas
Headquarters
Indianapolis, Indiana
1994

Architectural Projects Honor Award
American Institute of Architects, New Jersey
Chapter
Taiwan National Museum of Pre-History
Taitung City, Taiwan
1994

Casebook #10 Award
Print Magazine
"Rome Reborn" Exhibition, the Library
of Congress
Washington, D.C.
1994

Commercial Space Design Encouragement Award
Japanese Society of Commercial Space
Designers
Fukuoka Hyatt Regency Hotel and Office
Building
Fukuoka, Japan
1994

Architectural Projects Honor Award
American Institute of Architects, New Jersey
Chapter
Private Residence
New Jersey
1992

Architectural Projects Honor Award
American Institute of Architects, New Jersey
Chapter
Villa Gables
Meerbusch, Germany
1992

Architectural Projects Honor Award
American Institute of Architects, New Jersey
Chapter
Denver Central Library
Denver, Colorado
1992

National Honor Award
American Institute of Architects
The Newark Museum
Newark, New Jersey
1992

American Academy of Arts and Letters
Inducted as Member of Institute
1991

Architectural Projects Honor Award
American Institute of Architects, New Jersey
Chapter
Emory University Museum of Art and
Archaeology Renovation
Atlanta, Georgia
1991

Architectural Projects Honor Award
American Institute of Architects, New Jersey
Chapter
The Aventine
La Jolla, California
1991

Architectural Projects Honor Award
American Institute of Architects, New Jersey
Chapter
Beach House
Malibu, California
1991

Architectural Projects Honor Award
American Institute of Architects, New Jersey
Chapter
Makuhari International Market
Makuhari, Chiba Prefecture, Japan
1991

Architectural Projects Honor Award
American Institute of Architects, New Jersey
Chapter
Engineering Research Center
University of Cincinnati
Cincinnati, Ohio
1991

Architectural Projects Honor Award
American Institute of Architects, New Jersey
Chapter
The Team Disney Building
Burbank, California
1991

Interiors **Magazine Awards**
Inducted into the Interior Design Hall of Fame
1991

New Jersey Governor's Pride Award
Walt Whitman Creative Arts Award
1991

Architectural Projects Honor Award
American Institute of Architects, New Jersey
Chapter
Fukuoka Hyatt Regency Hotel and Office
Building
Fukuoka, Japan
1990

Architectural Projects Honor Award
American Institute of Architects, New Jersey
Chapter
Walt Disney World® Dolphin Hotel
and Walt Disney World® Swan Hotel
Lake Buena Vista, Florida
1990

Architectural Projects Honor Award
American Institute of Architects, New Jersey
Chapter
The Newark Museum
Newark, New Jersey
1990

Award of Excellence
American Federation of Arts
Graphic Design
1990

Downtown NJ Excellence Award
Downtown New Jersey, Inc.
The Newark Museum
Newark, New Jersey
1990

New Jersey Business and Industry Association Award for Achievement
The Newark Museum
Newark, New Jersey
1990

I.D. Awards
International Design
Consumer Products; Swid Powell Candy Dish
1990

Institute of Business Designers Awards
AI Finestra and Oculus Chairs
1990

National Honor Award
American Institute of Architects
Clos Pegase Winery
Napa Valley, California
1990

Architectural Design Award
Progressive Architecture
Henry House
Rhinebeck, New York
1989

Architectural Design Award
Progressive Architecture
Walt Disney World® Dolphin Hotel
and Walt Disney World® Swan Hotel
Lake Buena Vista, Florida
1989

Architectural Projects Honor Award
American Institute of Architects, New Jersey
Chapter
Emory University Museum of Art and
Archaeology Renovation
Atlanta, Georgia
1989

Architectural Projects Honor Award
American Institute of Architects, New Jersey
Chapter
Sarah Lawrence College Sports Center
Bronxville, New York
1989

Design Award
American Institute of Architects, Eastern Ohio
Chapter
Historical Center for Industry and Labor
Youngstown, Ohio
1989

I.D. Awards
International Design
Consumer Products; Alessi Pepper Mill
1989

I.D. Awards
International Design
Furniture; Vorwerk Carpet
1989

Architectural Design Award
Progressive Architecture
Historical Center of Industry and Labor
Youngstown, Ohio
1988

Architectural Projects Honor Award
American Institute of Architects, New Jersey
Chapter
Walt Disney World® Dolphin Hotel
and Walt Disney World® Swan Hotel
Lake Buena Vista, Florida
1988

Design Award
American Institute of Architects, Mid-Florida
Chapter
Walt Disney World® Dolphin Hotel
and Walt Disney World® Swan Hotel
Lake Buena Vista, Florida
1988

Architectural Projects Honor Award
American Institute of Architects, New Jersey
Chapter
Clos Pegase Winery
Napa Valley, California
1987

Architectural Projects Honor Award
American Institute of Architects, New Jersey
Chapter
Shiseido Health Club
Tokyo, Japan
1987

Architectural Projects Honor Award
American Institute of Architects, New Jersey
Chapter
Sunar Furniture Showroom
London, U.K.
1987

Architectural Projects Honor Award
American Institute of Architects, New Jersey
Chapter
Sotheby's Apartment Tower
New York, New York
1987

Architectural Projects Honor Award
American Institute of Architects, New Jersey
Chapter
Henry Residence
Rhinebeck, New York
1987

Architectural Projects Honor Award
American Institute of Architects, New Jersey
Chapter
Bryan Hall, University of Virginia
Charlottesville, Virginia
1987

National Honor Award
American Institute of Architects
Emory University Museum of Art and
Archaeology Renovation
Atlanta, Georgia
1987

National Honor Award
American Institute of Architects
The Humana Building
Louisville, Kentucky
1987

Henry Hering Memorial Medal
American Sculpture Society
The Portland Building
Portland, Oregon
1986

Gold Plate Award
American Academy of Achievement
1986

Interiors Magazine Award
The Humana Building
Louisville, Kentucky
1986

Interiors Magazine Award
Emory University Museum of Art and
Archaeology Renovation
Atlanta, Georgia
1986

Architectural Projects Honor Award
American Institute of Architects, New Jersey
Chapter
The Humana Building
Louisville, Kentucky
1985

Architectural Projects Honor Award
American Institute of Architects, New Jersey
Chapter
Clos Pegase Winery and Residence
Napa Valley, California
1985

National Honor Award
American Institute of Architects
San Juan Capistrano Library
San Juan Capistrano, California
1985

Architectural Projects Honor Award
American Institute of Architects, New Jersey
Chapter
Stamford Mixed-Use Development
Stamford, Connecticut
1984

Silver Spoon Award
Boston University
1984

Furniture Design Award
Progressive Architecture
Sunar Side Chair
1983

Architectural Design Award
Progressive Architecture
Environmental Education Center
Liberty State Park, New Jersey
1983

Architectural Projects Honor Award
American Institute of Architects, New Jersey
Chapter
San Juan Capistrano Library
San Juan Capistrano, California
1983

Architectural Projects Honor Award
American Institute of Architects, New Jersey
Chapter
Environmental Education Center
Liberty State Park, New Jersey
1983

Architectural Projects Honor Award
American Institute of Architects, New Jersey
Chapter
Riverbend Music Center
Cincinnati, Ohio
1983

Euster Award
Miami, Florida
1983

Indiana Arts Award
1983

National Honor Award
American Institute of Architects
The Portland Building
Portland, Oregon
1983

Resources Council Commendations
Sunar Table
1982

Architectural Projects Honor Award
American Institute of Architects, New Jersey
Chapter
Sunar Furniture Showroom
Dallas, Texas
1982

Furniture Design Award
Progressive Architecture
Sunar Arm Chair
1982

Institute of Business Designers Awards
Sunar Casement Fabric
1982

Institute of Business Designers Awards
Sunar Lounge Chair
1982

National Honor Award
American Institute of Architects
Schulman House
Princeton, New Jersey
1982

Special Recognition Honor Award
American Institute of Architects, New Jersey
Chapter
1982

Designer of the Year
Interiors Magazine
1981

Architectural Projects Honor Award
American Institute of Architects, New Jersey
Chapter
San Juan Capistrano Library
San Juan Capistrano, California
1981

Architectural Projects Honor Award
American Institute of Architects, New Jersey
Chapter
Sunar Furniture Showroom
New York, New York
1981

***Interiors* Magazine Award**
Sunar Furniture Showroom
New York, New York
1981

Architectural Design Award
Progressive Architecture
Beach House
Loveladies, New Jersey
1980

Architectural Design Award
Progressive Architecture
Kalko House
Green Brook, New Jersey
1980

Architectural Design Award
Progressive Architecture
Plocek House
Warren, New Jersey
1980

Architectural Projects Honor Award
American Institute of Architects, New Jersey
Chapter
Sunar Furniture Showroom
New York, New York
1980

Architectural Projects Honor Award
American Institute of Architects, New Jersey
Chapter
Sunar Furniture Showroom
Houston, Texas
1980

Architectural Projects Honor Award
American Institute of Architects, New Jersey
Chapter
Railroad Station Addition and Renovation
New Jersey
1980

Architectural Projects Honor Award
American Institute of Architects, New Jersey
Chapter
Environmental Education Center
Liberty State Park, New Jersey
1980

**Arnold W. Brunner Memorial Prize in
Architecture**
American Academy of Arts and Letters
1980

Resources Council Commendations
Rug #1
1980

Architectural Design Award
Progressive Architecture
Fargo-Moorhead Cultural Center Bridge
Fargo, North Dakota and Moorhead, Minnesota
1979

National Honor Award
American Institute of Architects
Gunwyn Ventures Professional Office
Princeton, New Jersey
1979

Architectural Design Award
Progressive Architecture
Chem-Fleur Factory Addition and Renovation
Newark, New Jersey
1978

Architectural Design Award
Progressive Architecture
Warehouse Conversion: Graves Residence
Princeton, New Jersey
1978

Architectural Projects Honor Award
American Institute of Architects, New Jersey
Chapter
Private Residence
Aspen, Colorado
1978

Architectural Projects Honor Award
American Institute of Architects, New Jersey
Chapter
Schulman House
Princeton, New Jersey
1978

Architectural Projects Honor Award
American Institute of Architects, New Jersey
Chapter
Abrahams Dance Studio
Princeton, New Jersey
1978

Architectural Projects Honor Award
American Institute of Architects, New Jersey
Chapter
Fargo-Moorhead Cultural Center Bridge
Fargo, North Dakota and Moorhead, Minnesota
1978

Architectural Design Award
Progressive Architecture
Crooks House
Fort Wayne, Indiana
1977

Architectural Projects Honor Award
American Institute of Architects, New Jersey
Chapter
Warehouse Conversion: Graves Residence
Princeton, New Jersey
1977

Architectural Design Award
Progressive Architecture
Snyderman House
Fort Wayne, Indiana
1976

Architectural Projects Honor Award
American Institute of Architects, New Jersey
Chapter
Snyderman House
Fort Wayne, Indiana
1976

Architectural Projects Honor Award
American Institute of Architects, New Jersey
Chapter
Crooks House
Fort Wayne, Indiana
1976

Architectural Projects Honor Award
American Institute of Architects, New Jersey
Chapter
Alexander House
Princeton, New Jersey
1975

Architectural Projects Honor Award
American Institute of Architects, New Jersey
Chapter
Medical Office: Ear, Nose and Throat
Associates
Fort Wayne, Indiana
1975

National Honor Award
American Institute of Architects
Hanselmann House
Fort Wayne, Indiana
1975

Architectural Projects Honor Award
American Institute of Architects, New Jersey
Chapter
Union County Nature and Science Museum
Mountainside, New Jersey
1974

Architectural Projects Honor Award
American Institute of Architects, New Jersey
Chapter
Hanselmann House
Fort Wayne, Indiana
1973

Architectural Design Award
Progressive Architecture
Rockefeller House
Pocantico Hills, New York
1970

Architectural Projects Honor Award
American Institute of Architects, New Jersey
Chapter
Oyster Bay Town Plan
Oyster Bay, New York
1967

Rome Prize
Arnold W. Brunner Fellowship
American Academy in Rome
1960–1962

Exhibitions

"Unbuilt Cincinnati"
The Cincinnati Forum for Architecture and
Urbanism
Cincinnati, Ohio
1998

American Architecture Awards Exhibition
The Chicago Athenaeum
Chicago, Illinois
1998

**"It's New, Try It! Dutch Architecture and the
American Model"**
Netherlands Architecture Institute
Rotterdam, The Netherlands
1997

"Michael Graves Architect Recent Work"
Inaugural Exhibition, Dorothy and Lawson
Reed Gallery
The Aronoff Center for Design and Art
University of Cincinnati
Cincinnati, Ohio
1996

"Michael Graves Architect Recent Work"
Topeka and Shawnee County Library
Topeka, Kansas
1996

Selected Work
The Arts Council of Princeton
Princeton, New Jersey
1996

"Designed to a Tea"
The Chicago Athenaeum
Museum of Architecture and Design
Chicago, Illinois
1995

"The Architect & The Tea Kettle"
Philadelphia Museum of Art
Philadelphia, Pennsylvania
1995

Hunterdon Art Center
Clinton, New Jersey
1995

"Great Houses of the 20th Century"
Max Protetch Gallery
New York, New York
1994

Clark County Library Grand Opening
Las Vegas, Nevada
1994

Tajima Inc. Grand Opening
Tokyo, Japan
1994

**Institute for Theoretical Physics Dedication
Ceremony**
University of California, Santa Barbara
Santa Barbara, California
March 18, 1994

"Early Work"
Max Protetch Gallery
New York, New York
1993

**"Michael Graves, Architect: Buildings and
Projects"**
Pittsburgh Cultural Trust
Pittsburgh, Pennsylvania
1993

"Michael Graves, Drawings and Projects"
Stockton State College Art Gallery
Pomona, New Jersey
1993

"Designs for a Museum"
Kansas City Art Institute
Kansas City, Missouri
1992

"Five Architects: 20 Years Later"
University of Maryland
1992

**"Michael Graves: Architecture and Product
Design"**
Cheekwood Fine Arts Center
Nashville, Tennessee
1992

"Michael Graves: Drawings and Projects"
Mikimoto Hall
Tokyo, Japan
1992

Freehand Drawing exhibition
GA Gallery
Tokyo, Japan
1992

"91 GA International"
GA International
Tokyo, Japan
1991

"Chateaux Bordeaux"
Centre Georges Pompidou
Paris, France
1991

"Concept Drawings"
Nexus Foundation for Today's Art
Philadelphia, Pennsylvania
1991

"Denver Public Library"
Denver Art Museum
Denver, Colorado
1991

"Green"
Max Protetch Gallery
New York, New York
1991

"Michael Graves"
Academy and Institute of Arts and Letters
New York, New York
1991

**"The Art of Architectural Drawings and
Photography in America, 1959–1990"**
The Rye Arts Center
Rye, New York
1991

"The Dream of Egypt"
Centro Culteral Arte Contemporanea
Mexico City, Mexico
1991

"UVA Builds"
The University of Virginia
School of Architecture
Charlottesville, Virginia
1991

"Washington State Historical Society"
Washington State Historical Society
Tacoma, Washington
1991

"Architectural Drawings"
Michael Ingbar Gallery
New York, New York
1990

"Architecture as Art"
Michael Ingbar Gallery
New York, New York
1990

"Michael Graves"
Indianapolis Art League
Indianapolis, Indiana
1990

"Michael Graves"
Syracuse University
School of Architecture
Syracuse, New York
1990

"Small Town/Distinguished Architects"
Historical Society of Princeton
Princeton, New Jersey
1990

"The Art of Drawing"
Kunsternes Hus
Oslo, Norway
1990

"1989 International Design Review Exhibit"
The Design Council of the
San Francisco Bay Area
San Francisco, California and traveling
1989

"Art Forum '89"
Holman Hall Gallery
Trenton State College
Trenton, New Jersey
1989

"Design for the Wine Country"
Contract Design Center
San Francisco, California
1989

"Design USA"
United States Information Agency
Washington, D.C.
1989

"GA International '89"
Global Architecture Gallery
Tokyo, Japan
1989

"Granary Island Symposium and Exhibition"
Gdansk, Poland
1989

"In the Architect's Eye"
Plains Art Museum
Moorhead, Minnesota and traveling
1989

"Michael Graves"
Butler Institute of American Art
Youngstown, Ohio
1989

"Michael Graves"
Momochi District Apartment Building
Fukuoka, Japan
1989

"Michael Graves: 25 Years in Princeton"
Princeton Arts Council
1989

Kirby Arts Center, Lawrenceville School
Lawrenceville, New Jersey
1989

"Michael Graves: A Figurative Architecture"
Johnstown Art Museum
Johnstown, Pennsylvania
1989

"Michael Graves: Current Projects"
Washington Design Center
Washington, D.C.
1989

"New York Architecture"
Deutsches Architekturmuseum
Frankfurt, West Germany and traveling
1989

Blair Art Museum
Holidaysburg, Pennsylvania
1989

"Chateaux Bordeaux"
Centre Pompidou
Paris, France
1988

"Michael Graves"
University of Maryland
College Park, Maryland
1988

"Michael Graves: A Figurative Architecture"
Duke University Museum of Art
Durham, North Carolina
1988

"New Constructions"
Hunterdon Art Center
Clinton, New York
1988

"Pluralism in Contemporary Architecture"
Deutsches Architekturmuseum
Frankfurt, West Germany
1988

"The Coliseum Site Redevelopment"
New York, New York
1988

"The Experimental Tradition: 25 Years of American Architectural Competitions"
The Architectural League
New York, New York
1988

"Art by Number"
Bucks County Community College
Artmobile, Newtown, Pennsylvania
1987

"Cadres en l'Air"
Rennes, France
1987

"Designs for Living: Architects' Drawings from the Collection of Barbara Pine"
Northwestern University
Evanston, Illinois
1987

"GA International 1987"
Global Architecture Gallery
Tokyo, Japan
1987

"Galveston Arches"
Cooper-Hewitt Museum
New York, New York
1987

"Jewelry from the Collection of Cleto Munari"
Museum of Modern Art
Los Angeles, California and traveling
1987

"Michael Graves"
Archivolto Gallery
Beauborg, Paris, France
1987

"Michael Graves"
Hamilton College
Clinton, New York
1987

"Michael Graves"
University of Virginia
Charlottesville, Virginia
1987

"Michael Graves: Recent Work"
San Francisco Conservatory of Music
San Francisco, California
1987

"Portals: Points of Entry"
Valencia Community College
Orlando, Florida
1987

"The Phoenix Municipal Center Competition"
University of California at Los Angeles
Los Angeles, California
1987

"What Could Have Been: Unbuilt Architecture of the 80's"
World Trade Center
Dallas, Texas
1987

Permanent Installation
Metropolitan Gallery
The Portland Building
Portland, Oregon
1987

The American House
Berlin, West Germany
1987

"Architects/Designers/Planners for Social Responsibility Benefit"
Max Protetch Gallery
New York, New York
1986

"Chicago Art Exposition"
John Nichols Gallery
New York, New York
1986

"Faculty Work"
School of Architecture, Princeton University
Princeton, New Jersey
1986

"Galveston Arches"
John Nichols Gallery
New York, New York
1986

"GMHC Benefit"
Sotheby's
New York, New York
1986

"Michael Graves"
Ballenford Books
Toronto, Canada
1986

"Michael Graves"
Carleton College
Northfield, Minnesota
1986

"Michael Graves"
West Virginia University
Morgantown, West Virginia
1986

"Remaking America: New Uses, Old Places"
The Architectural League
New York, New York
1986

"The Chair Fair"
New York Architectural League
New York, New York
1986

"Three Recent Projects by Michael Graves"
Princeton University
Princeton, New Jersey
1986

United States Information Agency
Traveling exhibition
1986

"Art + Architecture + Landscape"
San Francisco Museum of Modern Art
San Francisco, California
1985

"Artists & Architects: Challenges in Collaboration"
Cleveland Center for Contemporary Art
Cleveland, Ohio
1985

"Collaboration"
New York Academy of Art
New York, New York
1985

"Designs for Living"
Neuberger Museum
State University of New York at Purchase
Purchase, New York and traveling
1985

"Four Centuries of Architectural Drawing"
New York City AIA Members Gallery
New York, New York and traveling
1985

"From the Permanent Collection: Etchings"
Bell Art Gallery
Brown University
Providence, Rhode Island
1985

"Furniture by Architects"
Metropolitan Museum of Art
New York, New York
1985

"Henry Hornbostel and Michael Graves"
Emory University Museum
Atlanta, Georgia
1985

"High Styles"
Whitney Museum of American Art
New York, New York
1985

"Intuition and the Woodblock Print"
John Nichols Gallery
New York, New York
1985

"Le Affinita Elettive"
Milan Triennale
Milan, Italy
1985

"Michael Graves"
Max Protetch Gallery
New York, New York
1985

"Michael Graves' Proposed Expanded Whitney Museum of American Art"
Whitney Museum of American Art
New York, New York
1985

"Michael Graves/Edward Schmidt/Raymond Kaskey: Figure in Architecture"
John Nichols Gallery
New York, New York
1985

"Michael Graves: Recent Projects"
Princeton Club of New York
New York, New York
1985

"Nouveaux Plaisirs d'Architectures"
Centre Pompidou
Paris, France
1985

"Skyline Stories: Coliseum Site Proposals"
The Architectural League
New York, New York
1985

"The Critical Edge"
Rutgers University
New Brunswick, New Jersey and traveling
1985

"The Humana Building"
Harvard Graduate School of Design
Cambridge, Massachusetts
1985

"Wrappings"
The Arts Council of Princeton
Princeton, New Jersey
1985

"Chicago Art Fair"
Max Protetch Gallery
Chicago, Illinois
1984

"Clos Pegase Winery and Residence"
School of Architecture
Princeton University
Princeton, New Jersey
1984

"Competitions"
Architecture and Design Support Group
Biltmore Hotel
Los Angeles, California
1984

"Die Revision der Moderne: Postmoderne Archtitektur 1960–1980"
Deutsches Architekturmuseum
Frankfurt, West Germany
1984

"Environmental Education Center"
Jersey City Museum
Jersey City, New Jersey
1984

"Graves Draws Gatsby"
Max Protetch Gallery
New York, New York
1984

"Illustrated/Animated"
Irvine Fine Arts Center
Irvine, California
1984

"Michael Graves"
The Wadsworth Athenaeum
Hartford, Connecticut
1984

"Michael Graves: Esquisse for Five Houses"
Global Architecture Gallery
Tokyo, Japan
1984

"Michael Graves: Projects at The Newark Museum"
The Newark Museum
Newark, New Jersey
1984

"New Jersey AIA Awards"
New Jersey Society of Architects
Atlantic City, New Jersey
1984

"Post-Modern Mannerisms"
Ettinger Gallery
Laguna Beach College of Art
Laguna Beach, California and traveling
1984

"The Language of Michael Graves"
Royal Institute of British Architects
Heinz Gallery
London, England
1984

"The Language of Michael Graves"
The Pennsylvania State University
University Park, Pennsylvania
1984

"Three Architects"
Hines Industrial Boston, Ltd.
University Place Gallery
Cambridge, Massachusetts
1984

Architecture Department Opening Exhibition
Museum of Modern Art
New York, New York
1984

Fine Art Fund Benefit
Cincinnati, Ohio
1984

Group Show
Zeppelin Gallery
Denver, Colorado
1984

Memphis Milano Collections
Milan, Italy and traveling
1984

"Architecture and Art"
Museum of Contemporary Art
Montreal, Ontario
1983

"Architecture and Silver"
Max Protetch Gallery
New York, New York and traveling
1983

"Architecture in Prints"
Pratt Graphics Center
New York, New York
1983

"Art et Batiment"
Musee de l'Art Contemporain
1983

"Beau Arch I"
Hampton Day School
Bridgehampton, New York
1983

"Center for the Visual Arts: Ohio State University"
Harvard University
Cambridge, Massachusetts
1983

"Contemporary Architecture"
Mercer County Community College
Trenton, New Jersey
1983

"Design Since 1945"
Philadelphia Museum of Art
1983

"Five Designs for a Center for the Visual Arts"
The Gallery at the Old Post Office
Cincinnati, Ohio
1983

"Follies, Architecture for the Late-twentieth Century Landscape"
Leo Castelli Gallery
New York, New York and traveling
1983

"Michael Graves"
Florida International University
Miami, Florida
1983

"Michael Graves"
Galerie Piranesi
Zurich, Switzerland
1983

"Michael Graves""
Max Protetch Gallery
New York, New York
1983

"Michael Graves' Progressive Architecture Design Awards"
Lorenz & Williams
Dayton, Ohio
1983

"Michael Graves: Drawings, Furniture, and Textiles"
Moosart International
Miami, Florida
1983

"Ornamentalism"
Harcus Gallery
Boston, Massachusetts
1983

"Ornamentalism"
Hudson River Museum
New York, New York and traveling
1983

"The Architectural Impulse"
Tweed Gallery
Plainfield, New Jersey
1983

"The Humana Competition"
National Building Museum
Washington, D.C.
1983

"The Language of Michael Graves"
Moore College of Art
Philadelphia, Pennsylvania
1983

"The New American Architecture"
Sweet Briar College
Sweet Briar, Virginia
1983

"The Portland Building"
Colby College
Waterville, Maine
1983

"Travel Sketches by Architects"
Philippe Bonnafont Gallery
San Francisco, California
1983

"Window Room Furniture"
Tokyo and Osaka, Japan
1983

"Works in Progress"
Form and Function Gallery
Atlanta, Georgia
1983

Galeria Ynguanzo
Madrid, Spain
1983

Inaugural Exhibition
Zeppelin Gallery
Denver, Colorado
1983

Sunar Pavilion
Tulane University
New Orleans, Louisiana
1983

"At Home with Architecture"
University of California at San Diego
San Diego, California
1982

"Columns"
Cooper-Hewitt Museum
New York, New York
1982

"Decorative Screens"
Rizzoli Gallery
New York, New York
1982

"Memphis, Milan"
Furniture of the Twentieth Century
New York, New York
1982

"Michael Graves"
Northern Illinois University
DeKalb, Illinois
1982

"Michael Graves: Three Projects"
Rice University Gallery
Houston, Texas
1982

"New American Art Museums"
Whitney Museum of American Art
New York, New York
1982

"San Juan Capistrano Library"
Schindler House
Los Angeles, California
1982

"Shape and Environment: Furniture by American Architects"
Whitney Museum of American Art
Fairfield County, Connecticut
1982

"The Portland Building"
Inaugural Exhibition
Portland, Oregon
1982

"The Portland Building"
Institute for Architecture and Urban Studies
New York, New York
1982

"Venice Biennale, Strada Novissima"
San Francisco, California
1982

Textile Pavilion for Alcantara
Milan, Italy
1982

"Architettura/Idea"
XVI Milan Triennale
Milan, Italy
1981

"Artists & Architects Collaboration"
Traveling throughout the U.S.A.
1981

"Four International Masters"
Vesti Fine Arts Gallery
Boston, Massachusetts
1981

"Furniture by Architects"
Massachusetts Institute of Technology
Cambridge, Massachusetts
1981

"Inside Spaces"
Museum of Modern Art
New York, New York
1981

"Memphis Furniture"
Milan, Italy
1981

"Michael Graves"
Carolyn Schneebeck Gallery
Cincinnati, Ohio
1981

"Michael Graves: Five Projects"
Philadelphia Chapter AIA
Philadelphia, Pennsylvania
1981

"Michael Graves: Sketchbooks"
University of Witwatersrand
Johannesburg, South Africa and traveling
1981

"Michael Graves: Works in the West"
University of Southern California
Los Angeles, California
1981

"Speaking a New Classicism: American Architecture Now"
Smith College
Northampton, Massachusetts and traveling
1981

"Working Drawings"
Hunter College
New York, New York
1981

"Architects as Artists"
Rosa Esman Gallery
New York, New York
1980

"Architecture: Visionary and Imaginative"
State College of New York at Cortland
Cortland, New York
1980

"Art—Architecture"
Ohio State University
Columbus, Ohio
1980

"cARTography"
John Michael Kohler Art Center
Sheboygan, Wisconsin
1980

"Collage/Assemblage"
Summit Art Center
Summit, New Jersey
1980

"Creation and Recreation: America Draws"
Museum of Finnish Architecture
Helsinki, Finland and traveling throughout Europe
1980

"Dessins d'Architectes"
Galerie Nina Dausset
Paris, France
1980

"Forum Design"
Linz, Austria
1980

"Michael Graves"
Montclair Art Museum
Montclair, New Jersey
1980

"Michael Graves: Current Work"
Max Protetch Gallery
New York, New York and traveling
1980

"Michael Graves: Sketchbooks"
School of Architecture
University of Maryland
College Park, Maryland
1980

"Spectacular Spaces"
Cooper-Hewitt Museum
New York, New York
1980

"The Pluralist Decade"
Institute for Contemporary Art
Philadelphia, Pennsylvania
1980

"The Pluralist Decade"
Venice Biennale
Traveling throughout Europe
1980

"Art and Architecture: Space and Structure"
Protetch-McIntosh Gallery
Washington, D.C.
1979

"New Jersey Currents"
Summit Art Center
Summit, New Jersey and traveling
1979

"Transformations in Modern Architecture"
Museum of Modern Art
New York, New York
1979

"Architecture: Service, Craft, Art"
Rosa Esman Gallery
New York, New York
1978
Trenton State Museum
Trenton, New Jersey
1978

"Collage"
Goddard-Riverside Community Center
New York, New York
1978

"Roma Interrotta"
Rome, Italy
1978

"Artists' Postcards"
The Drawing Center
New York, New York
Touring under auspices of Smithsonian Institute
1977

"Beyond the Modern Movement"
Harvard University, Cambridge, Massachusetts
1977

"Drawing Toward a More Modern Architecture"
The Drawing Center
New York, New York
1977
Otis Art Institute
Los Angeles, California
1977

"Michael Graves, Projects 1967–1976"
Columbia University
New York, New York
Princeton University
Princeton, New Jersey
1976
University of California at Los Angeles
Kent State University
Kent, Ohio
University of Virginia
Charlottesville, Virginia
1977

"Two Hundred Years of American Architectural Drawing"
The Cooper-Hewitt Museum
New York, New York
1977
Jacksonville Art Museum
Jacksonville, Florida
Chicago Art Institute
Chicago, Illinois
Amon Carter Museum
Fort Worth, Texas
1978

Group Show
Grafica 80—Architettura
Milan, Italy
1977

"1975 AIA Honor Awards"
Kimbell Art Museum
Fort Worth, Texas
1976

"Architectural Studies and Projects"
Museum of Modern Art
New York, New York
1975

"Five Architects"
Castel Nuovo
Naples, Italy
1975

"The New York Five"
Art Net
London, England
1975

"Architectural Drawing"
Hewlett Gallery, Carnegie Mellon University
Pittsburgh, Pennsylvania
1974

"Architectural Drawing"
Institute for Architecture and Urban Studies
New York, New York
1974

"Due Architetti"
Michael Graves and Richard Meier
USIS Gallery
Milan, Italy
1974

"Five Architects"
School of Architecture and Urban Planning
Princeton University
Princeton, New Jersey
1974

Hanselmann House
University of Texas
Austin, Texas
1974

Birch Burdette Long Memorial Drawing Exhibition
The Architectural League of New York
New York, New York
1973

XV Triennale
Milan, Italy
1973

"Architecture of Museums"
Museum of Modern Art
New York, New York
1968

"The New City: Architecture and Urban Renewal"
Museum of Modern Art
New York, New York
Co-sponsored by the City of New York
1967

"The Union County Nature and Science Museum"
School of Architecture and Urban Planning
Princeton University
Princeton, New Jersey
1967

"40 Under 40"
The Architectural League of New York
The American Federation of the Arts
1966

Chronological List of Buildings, Projects, and Competitions

* Indicates work featured in this book
(see Selected Works)

Oyster Bay Town Plan
Oyster Bay, New York
1966

Hanselmann House
Fort Wayne, Indiana
1967–1968

Union County Nature and Science Museum
Mountainside, New Jersey
1967–1971

The Newark Museum Master Plan
Newark, New Jersey
1968

Benacerraf House
Princeton, New Jersey
1969

Rockefeller House
Pocantico Hills, New York
1969

Drezner House
Princeton, New Jersey
1970

Medical Office: Ear, Nose and Throat Associates
Fort Wayne, Indiana
1971

Keeley Guest House
Princeton, New Jersey
1972

Snyderman House
Fort Wayne, Indiana
1972

Gunwyn Ventures Professional Office
Princeton, New Jersey
1972

Alexander House
Princeton, New Jersey
1971 and 1973

Mezzo House
Princeton, New Jersey
1973

Wageman House
Princeton, New Jersey
1974

Claghorn House
Princeton, New Jersey
1974

Housing for the Elderly Competition
Trenton, New Jersey
1975

The Newark Museum Carriage House Renovation
Newark, New Jersey
1975

Crooks House
Fort Wayne, Indiana
1976

Schulman House
Princeton, New Jersey
1976

Graves Residence: The Warehouse
Princeton, New Jersey
1974–1992

Chem-Fleur Factory Addition and Renovation
Newark, New Jersey
1977

Fargo-Moorhead Cultural Center Bridge
Fargo, North Dakota and Moorhead, Minnesota
1977

Plocek House
Warren, New Jersey
1977–1982

Private Dance Studio
Princeton, New Jersey
1977

Private Residence
Green Brook, New Jersey
1978

Vacation House
Aspen, Colorado
1978

French and Company
New York, New York
1978

Railroad Station Addition and Renovation
New Jersey
1978

Beach House
Loveladies, New Jersey
1979

Apartment Renovation
New York, New York
1979

The Portland Building
Portland, Oregon
1980–1982

Red River Valley Heritage Interpretive Center
Moorhead, Minnesota
1980

Corporate Headquarters Competition: D.O.M.-Sicherheitstechnik
Bruhl, Germany
1980

11 Furniture Showrooms and Offices for Sunar-Hauserman
United States; London, U.K.
1980–1986

Apartment Building Conversion, Soho
New York, New York
1980

Environmental Education Center
Liberty State Park, New Jersey
1981–1983

Vassar College Art Department and Museum Addition Feasibility Study
Poughkeepsie, New York
1981

***The Humana Building**
Louisville, Kentucky
1982–1985

***The Newark Museum**
Newark, New Jersey
1982–1989 (Phases I and II); further renovations/additions ongoing

San Juan Capistrano Library
San Juan Capistrano, California
1982–1983

"Fire" Stagesets and Costumes
The Joffrey Ballet, New York
1982

"A Soldier's Tale" Stageset
Geulah Abrahams, Choreographer
1982

Emory University Museum of Art and Archaeology Renovation
Atlanta, Georgia
1982–1985

Matsuya Department Store Feasibility Study
Tokyo, Japan
1982

Republic Bank and Texas Theater Study
San Antonio, Texas
1982

St. James Townhouses
Cincinnati, Ohio
1982

Riverbend Music Center
Cincinnati, Ohio
1983–1984

Portico Square Townhouses
Philadelphia, Pennsylvania
1983

Glazer Farmhouse and Studio
McKinney, Texas
1983

Center for the Visual Arts, Ohio State University Competition
Columbus, Ohio
1983

Private Residence
Houston, Texas
1983

Alewife Center Office Building
Cambridge, Massachusetts
1983

Carriage House Renovation
New York, New York
1984–1987

Glendower Court Townhouses
Houston, Texas
1984

Glendower Court Residence
Houston, Texas
1984

Stamford Mixed Use Development
Stamford, Connecticut
1984

Erickson Alumni Center, West Virginia University
Morgantown, West Virginia
1984–1986

***Clos Pegase Winery**
Napa Valley, California
1984–1987

Canal Plaza Feasibility Study
Chandler, Arizona
1984

Diane Von Furstenberg Boutique
New York, New York
1984

*The Aventine
La Jolla, California
1985–1990

Grand Reef Master Plan
Galveston, Texas
1985

Princeton Hotel and Sporting Club
Princeton, New Jersey
1985

Columbus Circle Redevelopment
New York, New York
1985

Chamber Music Hall Addition, San Francisco
Conservatory of Music
San Francisco, California
1985

Sotheby's Apartment Tower
New York, New York
1985

Phoenix Municipal Government Center
Phoenix, Arizona
1985

Whitney Museum of American Art
New York, New York
1985–1988

Private Residence
Catskill Mountains, New York
1986

The Team Disney Building
Burbank, California
1986–1991

*The Crown American Building
Johnstown, Pennsylvania
1986–1989

Historical Center for Industry and Labor
Youngstown, Ohio
1986–1989

Shiseido Health Club
Tokyo, Japan
1986

Mardi Gras Arch
Galveston, Texas
1986

Ardleigh Crescent Townhouses
Hopewell, New Jersey
1986

South Carolina Marine Science Museum
Charleston, South Carolina
1986

Walt Disney World ® Resort Hotels Master Plan
Walt Disney World, Florida
1986

*Walt Disney World ® Resort Dolphin Hotel
Walt Disney World ® Resort Swan Hotel
Lake Buena Vista, Florida
1987–1990

*Bryan Hall
Charlottesville, Virginia
1987–1995

Sanders Dining Room
Princeton, New Jersey
1987–1988

Brisbane Civic and Community Center
Brisbane, California
1987

Henry House
Rhinebeck, New York
1987

Gateway Center Master Plan
Atlanta, Georgia
1987

The Sporting Club at the Bellevue Hotel
Philadelphia, Pennsylvania
1987–1989

Luisengarten and Braukessel Restaurants
Wüppertal, Germany
1987

St. Marks Church
Cincinnati, Ohio
1987

15 Stores and Galleries for Lenox China
United States; Frankfurt, Germany
1987–1990

*10 Peachtree Place
Atlanta, Georgia
1987–1991

*Portside Apartment Tower
Yokohama, Japan
1988–1991

Izumisano Center Competition
Izumisano, Japan
1988

Naiman Residence
La Jolla, California
1988

Daiei Office Building
Yokohama, Japan
1988

Metropolis Master Plan and Phase One Office
Building
Los Angeles, California
1988

*Momochi District Apartment Building
Fukuoka, Japan
1988–1989

Sarah Lawrence College Sports Center
Bronxville, New York
1988

Parc De Passy
Paris, France
1988

*Tajima Office Building
Tokyo, Japan
1988–1993

New Umeda City Master Plan
Osaka, Japan
1988

Columbus Convention Center
Columbus, Ohio
1988–1989

Dairy Barn Renovation
New Jersey
1988–1990

Hotel New York, Euro Disneyland
Villiers-Sur-Marne, France
1989–1992

Federal Triangle Development Site
Competition
Washington, D.C
1989

Royal Ichikai Golf Club
Tochigi Prefecture, Japan
1989

500-Forest Guest House
Susono, Shizuoka Prefecture, Japan
1989

The Tulips and the Elms
Brussels, Belgium
1989

Midousuji Minami Office Building
Osaka, Japan
1989–1990

Private Residence
Napa Valley, California
1990

The Detroit Institute of Arts Master Plan
and Renovations
Detroit, Michigan
Master plan 1990; renovations 1993 to present

*Engineering Research Center
Cincinnati, Ohio
1990–1995

*Institute for Theoretical Physics
Santa Barbara, California
1990–1994

*Clark County Library and Theater
Las Vegas, Nevada
1990–1994

*Kasumi Research and Training Center
Tsukuba City, Japan
1990–1994

*Fukuoka Hyatt Regency Hotel and Office
Building
Fukuoka, Japan
1990–1994

Onjuku Town Hall
Onjuku, Japan
1990–1993

*Beach House
Malibu, California
1990–1992

Manhattan Apartment
New York, New York
1990–

*Denver Central Library
Denver, Colorado
1990–1996

*Michael C. Carlos Museum
Atlanta, Georgia
1990–1993

Obihiro Mixed-Use Complex
Obihiro, Japan
1990

Isetan Department Store
Yokohama, Japan
1990

Private Residence
Sherman Oaks, California
1990

Private Residence
Neuilly, France
1990

Richard Stockton College Arts and Sciences Building
Pomona, New Jersey
1991–1996

Makuhari International Market
Makuhari, Japan
1991

NTT Corporate Headquarters Interiors
Tokyo, Japan
1991–1992

Competition for the Washington State Historical Society Museum
Tacoma, Washington
1991

Aoki Corporate Center Feasibility Study
Yokohama, Japan
1991

"Birth of Democracy"
The National Archives, Washington, D.C. and American School of Classical Studies
National Archives, Washington, D.C.
1991; 1993 installation

"Chateaux Bordeaux"
Centre Georges Pompidou
Paris, France
1991

Competition for the Texas Rangers Ballpark
Arlington, Texas
1991

Sany Building
Tokyo, Japan
1991

Indianapolis Art Center
Indianapolis, Indiana
1992–1996

Competition for the Herzlia Marina Master Plan
Herzlia, Israel
1992

Villa Gables
Meerbusch, Germany
1992

Trade Fair Installation
Frankfurt, Germany
1992

*Thomson Consumer Electronics Americas Headquarters
Indianapolis, Indiana
1992–1994

National Westminster Bank, Renovations and New Designs
New York and New Jersey
1992

Astrid Park Plaza Hotel and Business Center
Antwerp, Belgium
1992–1997

U.S. Federal Courthouse Renovation
Trenton, New Jersey
1992

Bayou Place Theater
Houston, Texas
1992

Competition for the Welsh National Center for Literature
Swansea, Wales, U.K.
1993

Competition for the Bass Museum
Miami Beach, Florida
1993

Ras Al Khaimah Cultural Center
Dubai, United Arab Emirates
Design 1993

*"Rome Reborn: The Vatican Library and Renaissance Culture"
The Library of Congress
Washington, D.C.
1993 installation

*Taiwan National Museum of Pre-History
Taitung City, Taiwan
1993–1999

Archdiocesan Center
Newark, New Jersey
1993–1995

*Nexus Momochi Residential Tower
Fukuoka, Japan
1993–1996

Competition for the Sarah Lawrence College Visual Arts Center
Bronxville, New York
1993

The South Pointe Design Charrette
Miami Beach, Florida
1993

United States Post Office
Celebration, Florida
1993–1996

*International Finance Corporation Headquarters
Washington, D.C.
1993–1997

*Castalia
The Hague, The Netherlands
1993–1998

Health, Fitness and Wellness Center, St. Paul's School
Concord, New Hampshire
1994

*Delaware River Port Authority
Camden, New Jersey
1994–1996

Competition for the Paradice Hotel and Casino
Las Vegas, Nevada
1994

Disney Garden Pavilions
Orlando, Florida
1994–1996

Pura-Williams Residence
Manchester-by-the-Sea, Massachusetts
1994–1997

Competition for the Postal and Telecommunications Building
Xiamen, China
1994

Jiang-to Boulevard Master Plan
Xiamen, China
1994

*1500 Ocean Drive and Ocean Steps
Miami Beach, Florida
1994–1999

Competition for the Marui Department Store
Tokyo, Japan
1994

Competition for the 42nd Street Hotel and Mixed-Use Development
New York, New York
1994

Competition for the Oakland Administration Building
Oakland, California
1994

*Saint Martin's College Library
Lacey, Washington
1995–2000

Topeka and Shawnee County Public Library
Topeka, Kansas
1995–2000

National Bank of Abu Dhabi Competition
Abu Dhabi, United Arab Emirates
1995

*Miramar Resort Hotel
El Gouna, Egypt
1995–1997

*Laurel Hall Student Residence
Newark, New Jersey
1995–1997

Cincinnati Ballpark and Stadium Complex
Cincinnati, Ohio
Design 1995

*Fujian Xingye Banking Tower
Shanghai, China
Design 1996

Alexandria Central Library
Alexandria, Virginia
1996–1999

U.S. Federal District Courthouse Annex
Washington, D.C.
1996–2002 annex; 2004 renovation

*O'Reilly Theater
Pittsburgh, Pennsylvania
1996–2000

*LIFE Magazine Dream House
1996

*Lake Hills Country Club
Seoul, Republic of Korea
1996–1997

*World Trade Exchange Center
Metro Manila, Philippines
Design 1996

*Miele Americas Headquarters
Princeton, New Jersey
1996–1999

Bryan Bergen House
Cincinnati, Ohio
1996–1998

Senopati Towers
Jakarta, Indonesia
1996

Uffelman House
Redding, Connecticut
1996–1999

*Ortigas Tycoon Twin Towers
Manila, Philippines
1996–1999

*El Gouna Golf Clubhouse and Restaurant
El Gouna, Egypt
1996–1999

Richardson International Center
Richardson, Texas
1996

Jasna Polana Dining Pavilion
Princeton, New Jersey
Design 1996

Drexel University Residence Hall
Philadelphia, Pennsylvania
1997–1999

Dongwha Hoiyhun Mixed-Use Project
Seoul, Republic of Korea
Design 1997

Hotel Makati
Makati, Philippines
Design 1997

Acacia Hotel
Taba Heights, Egypt
1997–1999

***NCAA 2000 Headquarters
and Hall of Champions**
Indianapolis, Indiana
1997–1999 Headquarters;
2000 Hall of Champions

*The Arts Council of Princeton
Princeton, New Jersey
Design 1997

*El Gouna Golf Villas
El Gouna, Egypt
1997–1999

*El Gouna Golf Hotel
El Gouna, Egypt
1997–1999

**Rearrangement of the Choir of the Cathedral
of Santa Maria del Fiore**
Florence, Italy
1997

*Fortis/AG Headquarters
Brussels, Belgium
1997–2002

French Institute/Alliance Française Library
New York, New York
1997–1998

Fukuoka 4th Building
Fukuoka, Japan
Design 1997

Intercontinental Hotel
Taba Heights, Egypt
1997–2000

North Area of Ogoori Station
Ogoori, Yamaguchi Prefecture, Japan
1997

*Peek & Cloppenburg Department Store
Düsseldorf, Germany
1997–1998

*Cotton Bay Resort Hotel Competition
Eleuthera, Bahamas
1998

***Main Library of Nashville and Davidson
County**
Nashville, Tennessee
1998

New Jersey Institute of Technology Master Plan
Newark, New Jersey
1998–1999

Impala Building
New York, New York
1998–2000

*The Washington Monument Restoration
Washington, D.C.
1998–2000

Century Tower
New York, New York
Design 1998

Cincinnati Art Museum Master Plan
Cincinnati, Ohio
Design 1998

Selected Bibliography

Articles

Allen, Jenny. "The 1996 LIFE Dream House." *LIFE* (May 1996).

"Architecture: The American Academy's Rare Book Room: A Michael Graves Design Enhances Preservation in Rome." *Architectural Digest* (December 1996).

Bedarida, Marc. "Euro Disney Park." *ARCH Plus* (December 1992).

Branch, Mark Alden. "Design Feature: Fish Story." *Progressive Architecture* (October 1990).

Branch, Mark Alden. "Story Time." *Progressive Architecture* (March 1990).

Brown, Patricia L. "At Home with Michael Graves: How the Pearl Designed his Oyster." *New York Times* (March 14, 1996).

Brown, Patricia L. "Disney Deco." *New York Times Magazine* (April 8, 1990).

Byron, Elizabeth S. "The Prince of Princeton." *HG* (July 1988).

Currimbhoy, Nayana. "Roman Holiday." *Interiors* (October 1990).

Faiferri, Massimo. "Two Recent Works by Michael Graves." *Industria delle Costruzioni* (December 1994).

Filler, Martin. "A Shrine to Wine." *House & Garden* (September 1987).

"Fukuoka Hyatt Regency Hotel." (In Japanese.) *Shoten Kenchiku* (August 1993).

Fukuwatari, Isao. "The Tajima Building." (In Japanese.) *Shin-kenchiku* (July 1994).

Gandee, Charles K. "Humana." *Architectural Record* (August 1985).

Glueck, Grace. "A 'Yellow Brick Road' Brightens a Museum." *New York Times* (November 12, 1989).

Goldberger, Paul. "A Little Book That Led Five Men to Fame." *New York Times* (February 11, 1996).

Goldberger, Paul. "A Remembrance of Visions Pure and Elegant." *New York Times* (January 3, 1993).

Goldberger, Paul. "And Now, an Architectural Kingdom." *New York Times Magazine* (April 8, 1990).

Goldberger, Paul. "Architecture of a Different Color." *New York Times Magazine* (October 10, 1982).

Goldberger, Paul. "Raising the Architectural Ante in California." *New York Times* (October 14, 1990).

Goldberger, Paul. "Rural Revisited: Working Wonders on a New Jersey Farm Property." *Architectural Digest* (May 1994).

Gomez, Edward M. "Graves' Progress." *Metropolitan Home* (March/April 1996).

Gorman, Jean. "Florida." *Interiors* (May 1994) (Walt Disney World, Florida).

Graaf, Vera. "Zeitgeist und Biedermeier." *Architektur & Wohnen* (February 1991).

Hamano, Yasuhiro. "Onjuku Town Hall and Health Center." (In Japanese.) *Shin-kenchiku* (July 1993).

Henderson, Justin. "California." *Interiors* (May 1992) (Team Disney Building, Burbank, California).

Hensler, Kate. "International Finance Corporation Headquarters." *Interiors* (May 1998).

Hoyt, Charles. "Hyatt Regency Hotel." *Architectural Record* (October 1996).

Hoyt, Charles. "Joining Hands to Connect a Campus." *Architectural Record* (July 1996).

Jodidio, Philip. "Euro Disney, le pari et le reve." *Connaissance des Arts* (April 1992).

Jordy, William H. "Aedicular Modern 6: The Architecture of Michael Graves." *New Criterion* (October 1983).

Kent Dorris, Virginia. "Surviving Value Engineering." *Architecture* (March 1994).

Meggs, Philip B. "Rare Show." *Print* (March/April 1993).

"Men of the Year." *GQ* (November 1997).

"Michael Graves." *Monthly Design* (December 1996).

"Momochi District Apartment Building." *Architektur + Wettbewerbe* (September 1991).

Papademetriou, Peter. "Four Not-so-easy Pieces." *Progressive Architecture* (March 1990).

Pastier, John. "An Intimate Sequence of Spaces." *Architecture* (December 1989).

Powell, Kenneth. "The Warehouse, Princeton, USA." *Country Life* (April 20, 1995).

Prisant, Carol. "Graves' New World." *World of Interiors* (May 1995).

Rozhon, Tracie. "Michael Graves: The Prince of Princeton." *Graphis* 312 (vol. 53, November/December 1997).

Rozhon, Tracie. "The House is in the Mail." *New York Times* (House & Home Section, July 2, 1998).

Russell, Beverly. "The Hotel New York." *Interiors* (May 1992).

Russell, John. "Architect Gives a Library Space to Read and Dream." *New York Times* (Wednesday, November 4, 1998).

Sala, Delia. "Fukuoka Hotel and Office Building." *Habitat Ufficio* (August/September 1994).

Schreiner, Judy. "Irrepressible Michael Graves." *Engineering News Record* (September 6, 1990).

Smith-Warren, Katherine. "Civic Architecture Takes a Right Turn: Denver's Library Competition." *Competitions* (Summer 1991).

Stanton, Melissa. "The 1996 LIFE Dream House by Michael Graves." *LIFE* (May 1997).

Stein, Karen D. "Gravesian Images." *Architectural Record* (February 1990).

Stein, Karen D. "On the Waterfront." *Architectural Record* (October 1986).

Sutro, Dirk. "Classical Animation." *Architecture* (June 1991).

Szabo, Brenda Dyer. "Midousuji Minami Office Building, Osaka." *Habitat Ufficio* (December 1993).

Tsuda, Margaret. "Four Buildings—One Museum." *Christian Science Monitor* (April 9, 1990).

Viladas, Pilar. "Full Circle." *Progressive Architecture* (September 1985).

Viladas, Pilar. "Mickey the Talent Scout." *Progressive Architecture* (June 1988).

Viladas, Pilar. "The Taste of a Tastemaker." *Progressive Architecture* (September 1988).

Wang, Li. "Architectural Visions." *Trenton Times* (March 29, 1998).

Weinstein, Sheryl. "Villa Graves." *Star-Ledger* (Home & Garden section, September 16, 1998).

Yoshihara, Yuki. "ARTE Yokohama." (In Japanese.) *Fusion Planning* (December 1992).

Books

Arnell, Peter & Ted Bickford (eds). *A Tower for Louisville: The Humana Competition.* New York: Rizzoli International Publications, 1982.

Bertsch, Georg Christof. *Der Wasserkessel von Michael Graves.* Frankfurt am Main: Design-Klassiker Verlag form, 1997.

Brown, Theodore L. & Maurizio De Vita (eds). *Michael Graves: Idee e projetti 1981–1991.* Milan: Electa, 1991.

Buck, Alex & Matthias Vogt (eds). *Designer Monographs 3: Michael Graves.* Berlin: Ernst & Sohn, 1994.

Carpenter, Edward K. *Print Casebooks 10: The Best in Exhibition Design.* Rockville, MD: RC Publications, 1994.

Collins, Michael & Andreas Papadakis. *Post Modern Design.* New York: Rizzoli International Publications, 1989.

Dunster, David (ed.). *Michael Graves.* London: Academy Editions, 1979.

Fleischmann, Melanie. *In the Neoclassic Style.* New York: Thames & Hudson, 1988.

Gebhard, David & Deborah Nevins. *200 Years of American Architectural Drawing.* New York: Whitney Library of Design for the Architectural League of New York and The American Federation of Arts, 1977.

Jencks, Charles. *Kings of Infinite Space: Michael Graves and Frank Lloyd Wright.* London: Academy Editions, 1984.

Jencks, Charles. *The Language of Post Modern Architecture.* London: Academy Editions, 1977.

Jensen, Robert & Patricia Conway. *Ornamentalism: The Return of Decorativeness in Modern Design and Art.* New York: C.N. Potter, 1982.

King, Carol Soucek. "Cloistered Classic." In *Empowered Gardens: Architects and Designers at Home.* PBC International, Inc., 1997.

Lebowitz, Fran. "The Warehouse." In *Building Sights,* edited by Ruth Rosenthal & Maggie Toy. London: Academy Editions, 1995, pp. 100–105.

Merkel, Jayne. *Michael Graves and the Riverbend Music Center.* Cincinnati: Contemporary Arts Center, 1987.

The Museum of Modern Art, New York. *Five Architects: Eisenman, Graves, Gwathmey, Hejduk, Meier.* New York: The Museum of Modern Art and Oxford University Press, 1975.

Myerson, Jeremy. "The Denver Central Library." In *New Public Architecture.* London: Laurence King Publishing, 1996.

Nichols, Karen Vogel, Patrick J. Burke & Caroline Hancock (eds). *Michael Graves: Buildings and Projects 1982–1989.* New York: Princeton Architectural Press, 1990.

Nichols, Karen, Lisa Burke & Patrick Burke (eds). *Michael Graves: Buildings and Projects 1990–1994.* New York: Rizzoli International Publications, 1995.

Pearman, Hugh. *Contemporary World Architecture.* London: Phaidon Press, 1998.

Poling, Clark V. *Henry Hornbostel/Michael Graves.* Atlanta: Emory University Museum of Art and Archaeology, 1985.

Powell, Kenneth. *Michael Graves: The Warehouse.* London: Phaidon Press, 1995.

Riewoldt, Otto. *Intelligent Spaces: Architecture for the Information Age.* London: Laurence King Publishing, 1997.

Shoshks, Ellen. *The Design Process.* New York: Whitney Library of Design, 1989.

Spencer, Dorothy. *Total Design: Objects by Architects.* San Francisco: Chronicle Books, 1991.

Stephens, Suzanne et al. (eds). *Building the New Museum.* New York: The Architectural League of New York, 1986.

Stern, Robert A.M. *New Directions in American Architecture.* New York: George Braziller, 1977.

Tapert, Annette. *Swid Powell: Objects by Architects.* New York: Rizzoli International Publications, 1990.

Turner, Judith. *Judith Turner Photographs Five Architects.* New York: Rizzoli International Publications, 1980.

University of Maryland. *Five Architects: Twenty Years Later.* Introduction by Steven W. Hurtt. College Park: University of Maryland, 1992.

Wheeler, Karen Vogel, Peter Arnell & Ted Bickford (eds). *Michael Graves: Buildings and Projects 1966–1981.* New York: Rizzoli International Publications, 1983.

Wheeler, Karen Vogel, Peter Arnell & Ted Bickford (eds). *Michael Graves: Obras Y Projectos 1966–1985.* Barcelona: Editorial Gustavo Gili, 1986.

Williams, Donald & Barbara Vance Wilson. Shaping Architecture for the Future: Michael Graves (b. 1934)." In *From Caves to Canvas: An Introduction to Western Art,* 2nd ed. Sydney, Australia: McGraw-Hill Book Company, 1998.

Zevon, Susan. "Pioneering Postmodernism." In *Inside Architecture,* 1996.

Writings and Interviews

Graves, Michael. "A Case for Figurative Architecture." In *Michael Graves: Buildings and Projects 1966–1981* by Karen Vogel Nichols, Patrick J. Burke & Caroline Hancock (eds). New York: Rizzoli International Publications, 1983.

"A Conversation with Michael Graves." Interview by John R. Kirk. *Modulus: The Architectural Review of the University of Virginia.* New York: Princeton Architectural Press, 1989.

Graves, Michael. "Has Post-modernism Reached its Limit?" *Architectural Digest Supplement* (April 1988).

"Humana Building a Louisville." *Paesaggio urbano* (July–October 1996).

Graves, Michael. "Le Corbusier's Drawn References." In *Le Corbusier: Selected Drawings.* London: Academy Editions, 1981.

"Michael Graves." *Architectural Drawing: The Art and the Process* by Gerald Allen & Richard Oliver (eds). New York: Whitney Library of Design, 1981.

"Michael Graves." Interview by Gordon Simmons. *Practices: Journal of the Center for the Study of the Practice of Architecture, University of Cincinnati* (vol. 2 , Spring 1993).

"Michael Graves." Interview by Stanley Collyer. *Competitions* (Winter 1994).

Graves, Michael. "Michael Graves." In *Speaking a New Classicism: American Architecture Now.* Smith College Museum of Art, 1981.

Graves, Michael. "The Necessity of Drawing: Tangible Speculation." *Architectural Design* (June 1977).

Graves, Michael. "Porta Maggiore." *Roma Interrota Incontri Internazionale d'Arte.* (Rome, 1978).

Graves, Michael. "Reading Edward Schmidt." Introductory essay for the Edward Schmidt Catalogue, Contemporary Realist Gallery, February 1996.

Graves, Michael. "Referential Drawings." *Journal of Architectural Education* (September 1978).

Graves, Michael. "Representation." In *Representation and Architecture* by Omer Akin & Eleanor F. Weinel (eds). Information Dynamics, 1982.

Graves, Michael. "Thought Models." *Great Models: North Carolina State School of Design* (Fall 1978).

"Toward Reading an Architecture." Interview by Douglas Ely. *Nassau Literary Review* (Princeton University, Spring 1978).

Graves, Michael. "The Wageman House and the Crooks House." In *Idea as Model.* New York: Institute for Architecture and Urban Studies and Rizzoli International Publications, 1981.

Graves, Michael. "The Window." In *Let's Open a Window into the Third Millennium.* SOMFY International Symposium, Dublin, 1993.

Acknowledgments

This monograph was produced largely through the extraordinary efforts of Dodie Colavecchio of Michael Graves & Associates' Communications Department. Other participants included Karen Nichols, who oversaw the contents and presentation; Caroline Hancock and Patrick Burke, who provided editorial assistance; Marek Bulaj, Janna Israel, and Adam Graves. who provided assistance with photographic images; and Annatina Schneider, who prepared many of the drawings of plans and sections.

Of course, over many years, the firm has appreciated the participation of staff members, too numerous to mention here, who have assisted Michael Graves and the firm's other Principals with the design and production of the projects included in this monograph.

Michael Graves & Associates would like to thank Paul Latham and Alessina Brooks of The Images Publishing Group for the opportunity to participate in the Master Architect Series and for their patience and cooperation during the course of preparing this volume.

The following firms and individuals have collaborated with Michael Graves & Associates on the projects represented in this monograph:

1717 Design Group
Atelier d'Art Urbain
Clark Associates
ECADI
Farmer Puckett Warner Architects, P.C.
Fukuoka Jisho Co., Ltd.
Fukuwatari & Architectural Consultants, Inc.
Grabowsky & Poort BV
Haigo Shen & Associates
Haldeman, Powell + Partners
Ahmed Hamdi, Architect
John Carl Warnecke & Associates
JMA Architects and Engineers
Kozo Keikaku Engineering
Klipp Colussy Jenks DuBois Architects, P.C.
Vlastimil Koubek, AIA
Kunwon International, Inc.
KZF Inc.
Langdon Wilson Architecture Planning
Alan Lapidus Architects, P.C.
Maeda Construction Company, Ltd.
Maeda Corporation
Massive Design Group
Okano Architectural Company, Ltd.
Orascom Touristic Establishments
Rami El Dahan & Soheir Farid Architects
Hildegard A. Richardson, AIA
Robert Swedroe, Architects & Planners
Schmidt Associates, Inc.
SERA Architects, P.C.
The Sigel Group
Smith, Hinchman & Grylls Associates, Inc.
The Tarquini Organization
Thomas, Miller & Partners
Wilson and Associates
Zenitaka Corporation

Photo Credits

Andrew Lautman: 48 (1); 49 (2); 50; 51 (4, 5); 52 (7); 53 (9); 54 (10, 11, 12)

AVEQ Fotografie, courtesy of MAB Groep B.V.: 56(1); 57 (5); 58 (10); 59 (16)

Courtesy Fukuoka Jisho Co. Ltd.: 104 (8); 207 (4)

Courtesy Maeda Corporation: 208; 209 (2, 3)

Courtesy MGA: 58 (9, 11); 74 (1, 2); 111 (11); 169 (3); 114 (28); 115 (30); 117 (3); 118 (6); 119 (11, 12, 13); 216 (1, 2, 3); 222 (10, 11)

Daniel Aubry: 106 (1, 2); 110 (12, 13, 14, 15); 112 (16, 17, 18, 19); 113 (20, 21, 22, 23, 24); 114 (25, 26, 27, 29); 115 (33)

Elizabeth Zeschin: 230; 232 (9)

Glen Cormier and Peter Malinowski/Insite: 78 (4)

Grant Mudford: 85 (4, 5); 86

Gregory Murphey: 44 (2, 4); 46 (6, 7, 9, 10)

Hewitt/Garrison: 78 (2); 80 (12); 82; 83 (14, 15, 16)

Isao Inbe: 204 (1); 205 (4)

Jeff Goldberg/ESTO, Disney characters © Disney Enterprises, Inc/Used by permission from Disney Enterprises, Inc.: 8 (4)

Joel Kelly: 33 (4)

John Connell: 77; 78 (1); 80 (9, 10, 11)

Marek Bulaj: 13 (1); 56 (2, 3); 58 (6, 7, 8); 59 (13, 14, 15); 60 (1); 62 (5); 64 (1, 2); 65 (4, 5, 6, 7, 8); 66 (1, 2, 3); 67 (4, 5, 6); 68 (1, 2); 69 (3); 70 (1, 2); 71 (3, 4, 5); 72 (6, 7); 73 (9); 75 (3, 4); 106 (3); 107 (4); 108 (5, 6, 7); 116 (1); 117 (4, 5); 118 (7, 9, 10); 119 (14, 15, 16, 17); 120 (3); 124 (2); 125 (3, 4); 126 (1, 2, 3); 127 (4, 5); 128 (1, 2); 129 (3); 130 (4); 131 (5); 146 (1); 150 (1); 160 (1, 2, 3, 4); 161 (5, 6, 7, 8); 162 (9, 10); 163 (11, 12, 13, 14, 15); 164 (1, 2, 3, 4); 166 (1, 2); 167 (3, 4, 5); 168 (12); 170 (1, 2, 3, 4); 171 (5, 6); 178 (1); 193 (10); 194 (2); 196 (5, 6); 197 (7); 199 (2); 210 (2, 3); 212 (4); 214 (6); 224 (1, 2); 226 (3, 4, 5); 227 (6, 7, 8); 229 (5)

Mark Fiennes: 228 (2); 229 (3); 234 (11); 235 (12)

Matt Wargo: 60 (2, 3); 61; 63 (7)

Moto Niki: 34 (3)

Motoi Niki/Nacása+Partners Inc.: 35 (5); 36; 37 (7)

Nacása + Partners Inc.: 98 (1); 105 (11)

Otto Baitz/ESTO: 84 (2); 85 (6); 87 (9, 10)

Paschall/Taylor: 8 (2); 16 (2); 17 (4); 18 (5); 19; 20 (9); 21 (11); 22 (14); 23 (15); 84 (1); 85 (3); 88–89

Paul Rocheleau: 231 (8)

Peter Aaron/ESTO: 13 (3); 16 (1); 17 (3); 20 (far left); 23 (16); 206 (1, 2, 3); 228 (1)

Peter Malinowski/Insite: 146 (2, 3, 5); 147 (6); 148 (7, 9); 149 (10, 11, 12); 182–183; 184 (2, 3); 185; 186 (7); 187 (8, 9); 203; 217; 218 (5); 219 (6); 221; 222–223

Philip Beaurline: 177; 178 (4, 5); 180; 181 (8, 9)

Proto/Acme Photo, used by permission from Disney Enterprises, Inc.: 8 (3)

Reproduced from Maeda Corporation "Blue Book": 104 (10)

Robert Faulkner: 198 (1); 199 (3, 4); 201 (7, 8)

Sadamu Saito: 42 (4, 5, 6)

Shinkenchiku-Sha: 34 (4)

SS Tokyo, Hirokazu Yokose: 14 (1); 38 (1, 2); 40–41; 43 (7)

Steven Brooke, used by permission from Disney Enterprises, Inc.: 8 (1); 90 (2); 92, 93 (5, 6); 94 (7, below); 95 (9); 96 (11), 97 (12, 13, 14, 15, 16)

Steven Brooke: 134 (1, 2); 135 (3); 136 (4, 5, 6); 137 (7); 138 (1, 2); 140; 141 (5, 6); 142–143; 144; 145 (9, 10); 173 (1, 2); 174 (3, 4, 5); 175 (7); 188 (1); 198 (2, 4, 6); 190–191; 192 (9)

Thorney Lieberman: 153 (6); 155 (8, 9, 11, 12); 159 (16, 17, 18, 19, 21)

Tim Hursley: 7; 24 (1); 24 (3); 25 (4); 26 (5); 27 (7); 28 (8, 9, middle); 29 (11, 12); 30–31; 133; 150 (2); 151 (3); 152 (4, 5); 156–157; 158 (15); 159 (20)

Toyota Photo Studio: 98 (2); 99 (3); 100; 101 (6); 102–103

Wilbur Montgomery: 44 (1, 3); 46 (5); 8

William Taylor: 34 (1); 79 (5, 6, 7, 8); 87 (8)

Yum, Seung Hoon: 120 (1, 2); 121; 122; 123 (6, 7, 8)

Index

Bold page numbers refer to featured projects.

Every effort has been made to trace the source of copyright material contained in this book. The publishers would be pleased to hear from copyright holders to rectify any errors or omissions.

The information and illustrations in this publication have been prepared and supplied by Michael Graves & Associates. While all reasonable efforts have been made to ensure accuracy, the publishers do not , under any circumstances, accept responsibility for errors, omissions and representations express or implied.